T0332435

"Nicaso and Danesi provide an excellent, empirically rich insight into the complexities of organized crime groups in the digital field. Their book is a refreshing and engaging addition to both cybercrime and organized crime literature."

—**Anita Lavorgna**, *Associate Professor, University of Bologna*

THE DARK MAFIA

This book explores how organized crime has adapted and evolved in sync with ever-expanding technologies to update its popular image and to conduct its covert operations. It shows how organized crime operates in dark virtual spaces and how it can now form a dynamic interactive system with legitimate online spaces, solidifying its criminal exploits and resources, and making them attractive to a new generation of computer users. Focusing on Italian Mafias, Russian and Georgian criminal groups and drug cartels, and Asian crime syndicates such as Yakuza and Triads, this book aims to describe and explain the reasons behind the continuity of online and offline crime, taking into consideration whether or not Internet culture has radically changed the way we perceive organized crime and if so how, and thus how the shift in popular imagery that the Internet has brought about affects its actual illegal activities. We also consider how organized crime has shifted its locale from the physical to the virtual, how cybercrime has allowed criminal organizations to adapt and reinvent themselves, and how the police now use technology against organized crime.

To better understand the new generation of criminals, it is becoming increasingly urgent to understand the latest technologies and how criminals utilize them. *The Dark Mafia* is an engaging and accessible introduction to understanding virtual organized crime. It will appeal to students and scholars of criminology, sociology, policing, and all those interested in the digital age of organized crime.

Antonio Nicaso is an internationally recognized organized crime expert, who has published more than 40 books on Mafia and Mafia-like criminal organizations, including *Bad Blood*, which inspired a major television series. He teaches Social History of Organized Crime and Mafia Culture and the Power of Symbols, Rituals and Myth at Queen's University, Canada.

Marcel Danesi is Professor Emeritus of Anthropology at the University of Toronto, where he taught a course on Forensic Semiotics for many years. He has authored *Organized Crime: A Cultural Introduction* (Routledge, 2021) along with Antonio Nicaso.

THE DARK MAFIA

Organized Crime in the Age of the Internet

Antonio Nicaso and Marcel Danesi

Routledge
Taylor & Francis Group

LONDON AND NEW YORK

Designed cover image: Marco_Piunti

First published 2023
by Routledge
4 Park Square, Milton Park, Abingdon, Oxon OX14 4RN

and by Routledge
605 Third Avenue, New York, NY 10158

Routledge is an imprint of the Taylor & Francis Group, an informa business

© 2023 Antonio Nicaso and Marcel Danesi

British Library Cataloguing-in-Publication Data
A catalogue record for this book is available from the British Library

ISBN: 978-1-032-24437-2 (hbk)
ISBN: 978-1-032-24436-5 (pbk)
ISBN: 978-1-003-27859-7 (ebk)

DOI: 10.4324/9781003278597

Typeset in Bembo
by Apex CoVantage, LLC

CONTENTS

FIGURES

ACKNOWLEDGMENTS

We are indebted to the following individuals for having provided us with important first-hand information via zoom interviews and who have sent us documents and other materials as part of the background research for this book: Francesco Messina, Central Anti-Crime Director of the Italian State Police; Ivano Gabrielli, Head of the Italian Postal and Communications Police, a unit of Italy's state police that investigates cybercrime; General Alessandro Barbera, former Chief of the Central Investigation Service on Organized Crime for the Guardia di Finanza; General Pasquale Angelosanto, Commander of ROS, a special operative group of Carabinieri; Maurizio Vallone, Head of Anti-Mafia Investigation Directorate, and many scholars, including Marcello Ravveduto, Professor of Contemporary History and Digital Public History at the Universities of Salerno and Modena-Reggio Emilia. We have incorporated their insights, words, and relevant materials throughout. Needless to say, all interpretations are our own and not necessarily those of our sources, as are any infelicities that our book may contain.

We sincerely hope that our book will "make a difference," as the cliché goes, raising awareness of how organized crime is still powerful and sinister in today's complex technological world. While it has moved to cyberspace, it has not changed its vicious nature. To cite an ancient Italian proverb, "a fox changes its fur, but not its habits." The

fox has indeed changed its fur and is now spreading its habits throughout the Internet, where it is acquiring new and more sinister ones.

Antonio Nicaso, *Queen's University*
Marcel Danesi, *University of Toronto*

INTRODUCTION

The 2020 movie *Capone* was a contemporary revisitation of the life of one of the most iconic American gangsters of the twentieth century, Al Capone. As interesting and insightful as it was, the film did not catch on broadly. It seems that the figure of the Hollywood-fashioned wise guy, with all his psychological baggage, had lost its luster, becoming an anachronistic trope in the public eye in the twenty-first century. The film was a nostalgic punctuation mark on the growing irrelevance of the figure of a ruthless, larger-than-life mobster who lived by a code of secrecy and allegiance to his clan. Capone belonged to a different era of mob glamorization perpetuated by movies and television programs. In the current Internet era, this figure has lost its resonance.

The movie raises a key question: Has organized crime truly receded to the margins of public interest, and if not, where does it stand? The main purpose of this book is to address this question, examining why and how organized crime has changed. To seek relevant answers, we have used four primary sources: the relevant academic literature dealing with organized crime in the current age; online journalistic reports, which have provided us with pertinent information on specific cases of current-day organized crime; the actual social media profiles and postings of members and alleged members of criminal organizations; and the insights and information provided to us by law enforcement officers working for Italian police forces, whom

DOI: 10.4324/9781003278597-1

we interviewed at length (see Acknowledgments). Also, we talked to investigators in North America, South America, Asia, and Europe, who preferred to remain anonymous.

Throughout this book, we will use organized crime and criminal groups as a term for any criminal organization, and gangs only for street and online cliques. The lower-case spelling of *mafia* and *mafias* will indicate any traditional criminal organization that exhibits parallel forms of behavior, illegal activities, and other structural features of the Sicilian Mafia, also known as Cosa Nostra, one of the most notorious crime groups in existence. Also, *mobster* and its plural form will be used as a synonym for members of any traditional criminal organization. Our approach reflects rationalist and culturalist frameworks, which emphasize the relation between criminal operations and cultural aspects of the organizations, rather than focusing only on market-based and profit-oriented organizations. In the development of Mafia and Mafia-like criminal organizations, it is the requirement of cultural identity that has always played a role in keeping them distinct as criminal groups – hence their use of symbols, myths, and rituals.

A starting point for grasping how organized crime has changed in the current age is February 2011, when a website called Silk Road became one of the first illegal drug markets on the Dark Web – the part of the World Wide Web that is not visible to search engines and requires the use of an anonymizing browser to be accessed. Soon, the website became a major global drug trafficking locale, with drugs purchased using cryptocurrency, which itself was almost untraceable. In October 2013, the website was finally shut down by the FBI; but this was not the end of the line for illegal marketplaces on the Dark Web. Other sites that offered similar services and products quickly replaced the Silk Road. Since then, a new regime of organized crime operating in cyberspace has spread throughout the globe, giving rise to what can be called "dark mafia." With this term, it is possible to define any criminal organizations operating in the dark regions of cyberspace, where the traditional illegal activities of organized criminal groups, from drug and sex trafficking to extortion and racketeering, are now either taking place, or being planned. What has happened to those complex organizations we define as mafias? Has their migration to online spaces signaled an irreversible paradigm shift in how they operate and how they are perceived by the general public and by themselves? Is organized cybercrime the reason why the wise guy is likely to be relegated to a bygone era, like the Capone character of the 2020 movie?

One thing is certain: mafia-type organizations have not disappeared; they have adapted to the new cognitive conditions and communicative environments brought about by the Internet revolution. But is it also true that its previous organicity of structure, along with its public image, has taken a veritable beating, fragmented increasingly by the world of algorithms and memes in which everyone is immersed today? In effect, are mafia-type organizations reconceptualizing their historically established codes and sense of ethnic or geographical identity to differentiate themselves from random crime groups? The ancient symbols, honor codes, and pseudo-narratives that mobsters have always spun about themselves are being revamped in an age of instant and ephemeral information, viral videos, and memes, whereby new narratives and revisions of history are emerging all the time. However, this new semiotic environment has hardly disrupted the main operations of organized criminals; it has actually enhanced them. What has changed is the self-styled idyllic view of mobsters as valiant knights, which they have been perpetuating for centuries and which they are updating in various ways in the new virtual environments. Mobsters are now dark figures operating in the recesses of the Dark Web (the hidden part of the Internet). Still, they are also putting themselves on display publicly on the surface Internet via social media profiles that they use to promote themselves and brag about their criminal achievements. In effect, the wise guy of the past, fashioned by Hollywood, has given way to the cool guy of the Internet, fashioned by young mafiosi themselves, also called "sympathetic perpetrators" (Renga, 2013). Organized criminal culture is nothing if not an adaptive one, evolving in sync with the ever-changing technologies, values, perceptions, and practices of the broader society, and using these to update not only its public image but also how it conducts its secretive operations. The Dark Web affords a new space where mafia-type organizations can hide with diminished fear of being discovered and carry out their criminal affairs much more efficiently and secretively than in any previous era in the real world. This contrastive dynamic between the secretive operations of the criminals on the Dark Web and the public exposure that they crave on the surface every day is *the* defining characteristic of mafias in cyberspace, a term introduced generally by William Gibson in his *Sprawl* trilogy. This split character that it exhibits can be called, simply, *dualistic*.

While we will focus on the different mafia and mafia-type organizations which originated in Italy (in most parts), we will reference other cyber-criminal groups for comparative reasons. As mentioned earlier, we will use the term *mafias* in the multiple related meanings that it evokes today but mainly as a general term for organized crime groups with similar characteristics of the Sicilian Mafia. We take this liberty not only because of terminological convenience but also because the term *mafia* itself is not used today by the Sicilian Mafiosi themselves, who prefer to refer to themselves as *Cosa Nostra*. This term emerged first in the United States in the 1960s during the interrogation of a former member of the Genovese crime family who turned state witness. Nevertheless, we are aware of the pitfalls of adopting this label in a general way. The anti-Mafia judge Giovanni Falcone, murdered by the Sicilian Mafia in 1992, objected strongly to the conflation of the term Mafia with organized crime in general (cited in Lupo, 2009: 1–2):

> While there was a time when people were reluctant to pronounce the word "Mafia." Nowadays people have gone so far in the opposite direction that it has become an overused term. I am no longer willing to accept the habit of speaking of the Mafia in descriptive and all-inclusive terms that make it possible to stack up phenomena that are indeed related to the field of organized crime but that have little or nothing in common with the Mafia.

We will thus use the term only for convenience, as just mentioned, even though we are well aware of its pitfalls, as Falcone so perceptively understood. Also, the lower-case spelling allows us to move away ontologically from older concepts of organized crime based on ethnicity, blood ties, and the like, to a broader designation for the term in the current age, as mobsters adapt to the advantages offered by cybercrime in favor of age-old business models and membership constraints based on personalization and geographical–cultural origins. This usage of the term actually started with the young mobsters themselves as they began to move up the ranks at the Millennium to take over the command positions. In several social media sites that we visited, belonging to the younger members of the different organizations – the Sicilian Mafia, the Calabrian 'Ndrangheta, and the Neapolitan Camorra – we noticed different kinds of self-referential terms, perhaps indicating that traditional terminologies are mutating semantically among the criminals themselves.

Since this semantic shift has occurred in the Web 2.0 world, mafia-type organizations today can be characterized collectively as "Mafia 2.0." The term is used also in reference to the emergence of a dualistic character – namely one that relates to the real world and the other to the so-called hyperreal one. The term *hyperreality* was coined by the late French philosopher Jean Baudrillard (1983), who defined it as the state of consciousness brought about by constantly looking at the images and content of screens, whereby people are conditioned to no longer distinguish or desire to distinguish, between real worlds and the imaginary one inside the screens.

The Internet is, in effect, a hyperreality-generating machine that has created a cognitive and social environment for the dualism to crystallize. This might explain, in part, why the secret codes and ethnic constraints of the traditional mafias may be on the wane to greater or lesser extent (depending on the organization) – they have no meaning in hyperreality. The strength of any past version of mafia culture has always been implanted on the emotional sway of a native soil, where it could claim a tangible and visible stake. In cyberspace, this has no significance, as we will see; and this seems to imply that the distinctive mafias of the past are becoming less visible entities. On the Dark Web, it does not matter if one is a Sicilian Mafioso, a Hells Angel member, or a Mexican drug cartel dealer. In the night, all cows become black, as Hegel aptly observed. Nonetheless, some criminal organizations continue to carry the weight of their traditional reputations, which have enormous value. All that matters is the operationality of the dark marketplaces and the advantages they afford to collaborative transnational syndication. Clearly, to better understand the new generation of mafia actors, it is becoming ever more relevant to understand the new technologies criminals are utilizing in hyperreality and how these affect their states of mind and their sense of identity.

What does the term mafias mean today, and what will it mean in the future? Like an optical illusion, mafia-type organizations appear and disappear in a continuous play of illusionary mirrors, which it uses as leverage against our ability to recognize them for what they are – a ruthless power-hungry organization which craves to control people and territories. They have always competed for power with legitimate states without entering into direct conflict with them, but by exploiting their weaknesses and short memories. Now the question becomes: How can mafia-type organizations, obsessed with remaining invisible, confront a networked world that instead thrives on visibility and exposure and in which the new generation of mafiosi now live? Mafias are nothing if not adaptive. They have turned their early mistrust of the Internet into a new operational system, moving both to the dark corners of the Internet to conduct its business and to the public world of social networks where mafiosi now show themselves off to the entire world. But even in the latter case, they use social media cleverly as their "eyes and ears" to keep a tab on their business 24 hours a day. It is in this networked universe that inter-clan and intra-clan complaints, problems, and controversies are presented, negotiated, and resolved and from where they can strengthen their grip over their victims through the psychological power of mind control that social media make available to them.

As researchers and writers on organized crime, we are somewhat surprised to find a paucity of monographic treatments dealing with the dualistic character organized crime has developed since the Silk Road illegal marketplace era. The wise guy image crafted by movies such as *The Godfather* has now been replaced by memetic images of mafiosi bragging and looking like everyone else on TikTok. This has not, however, changed the twisted criminal ethics of mobsters, who have strategically retained their fundamental core of criminal operationality. We have written our book in a style that we hope will be of interest to both those dealing with criminal matters professionally and general audiences alike. In each chapter we provide case studies (actual cases involving organized crime), which are intended to render the themes and theories espoused in the chapter concrete. Our book could thus also be used as a textbook for introducing and discussing organized cybercrime in different kinds of courses, including criminology, sociology, psychology, anthropology, and other social sciences. Since we include first-hand information provided to us by various authorities who are themselves fighting organized crime, we hope that our treatment will be as viable as possible.

1
THE MAFIA IN CYBERSPACE

Prologue

The 1999 movie *The Matrix* was a cautionary tale about the arrival of a new world order in which everyday life unfolded as much in the real world as on the computer screen. The film provided one of the first discerning perspectives of how the computer had changed the way we view everything (literally), from conversations to history and even reality. The movie's main protagonist, Neo, discovers that he lives on both sides of the computer screen and that his engagement with the world, himself, and others was shaped by that screen, whose technical name is the *matrix*. But the same word also meant "womb" in Latin. The movie's subtext was, clearly, that, with the advent of computers, humans are now born through two kinds of wombs – the biological and the technological.

The cognitive-communicative-interactional revolution that digital technologies have engendered has been impactful. The world of the matrix engages all of us in a dualistic dynamic with *reality* outside the screen and *hyperreality* inside it, as Baudrillard (1983) characterized such a world even before the advent of the Internet. Revealingly, a copy of his 1981 book, *Simulacra and Simulation*, was assigned by the directors of the movie to the actors before filming. Distinguishing between what is real and what is imaginary, Baudrillard claimed, has become moot, given that both are seamlessly blended

DOI: 10.4324/9781003278597-2

in a psychological environment wherein it is no longer necessary to differentiate between where one ends and the other begins. As Canadian communications theorist Marshall McLuhan (1968: 5) wrote long before the Age of the Internet (which he anticipated): "We live invested in an electric information environment that is quite as imperceptible to us as water is to fish." With this observation, McLuhan was already warning us that we tend to be unaware of the mental effects of the technologized systems in which we live. Like fish in water, we tend not to realize that the "water" shapes how we live and interact with each other within it. McLuhan designated the world that was emerging as the "global village," a connected world consisting of an enormous mass of information scattered in bits and pieces. As he so aptly observed: "Environments are not just containers but are processes that change the content totally" (McLuhan, 1962: 200).

The global village exists in what has come to be called *cyberspace*. As Rees-Mogg and Dale Davidson (1997: 8) have characterized it, cyberspace is powerful and empowering because it is "a virtual interactive experience that is accessible regardless of a geographic location." This virtual environment (on the other side of the screen) is now a locus for daily affairs, interactions, and businesses – including criminal ones. Cybercrimes have in effect become the primary form of criminality in the global village. Because they occur on the other side of the screen, the danger is that they are given less prominence and perhaps even importance unless one is victimized. Cyberspace thus provides the kind of protection from public scrutiny that real geographical space has never been able to offer to criminals, especially criminal organizations. Organized crime is indeed evolving, becoming ever more present on the screen. FBI director Christopher Wray (2018) has said, "As cyber threats evolve, we need to evolve as well." And, as Bruno Pavlicek (2020) has observed, this evolution has made previous approaches to the phenomenon of organized crime, investigative and scholarly, anachronistic:

> According to the United Nations Office of Drugs and Crime, organized cyber-criminals engage in a multitude of cyber-crimes to include but not limited to fraud, but various malware attacks, intellectual property theft, as well as the sale and distribution of counterfeit products (knock-offs). They also contract themselves out to provide services to other cyber-criminals to further facilitate their crimes, whether it be the manufacturing

of fake documents, selling of self-created malware, DDoS (Distributed Denial of Service) and botnet services, as well as phishing and key logger tools, just to name a few. As one can see, organized cyber-crime is anything but the traditional mafia that we all associate organized crime to be.

The primary goal of this book is to follow up concretely on Wray's observation, by dealing with organized cybercrime and how it has changed the rules of the criminal games that traditional mafias played in real spaces in the past. We start with an overview of the differences between real space and cyberspace criminality to provide a background to the remainder of the book, in line with previous work in this area (Button and Cross, 2017, Ruggiero, 2019, Lavorgna, 2020). Cybercrime rates, as Pavlicek suggested, are increasing at the same time that the rates for traditional criminality remain stable. Exploring how the two differ is particularly relevant to understanding the evolutionary nature of organized crime. As Maras (2014: 3) has pointed out, the main difference between real space criminality and cybercriminality is that the latter "knows no physical or geographic boundaries" and can thus be carried out with less effort, with greater ease, and at more incredible speeds than geographically constrained crime.

Mafia 1.0: Organized Crime in Real Space

Organized crime has been traditionally differentiated from the illegal acts committed by random "unorganized" criminals (thieves, muggers, spontaneous street cliques, and so on) by several traits, including the use of a distinctive moniker, a self-styled pseudo-history intended to locate the criminal organization in social reality, a set of working principles for the commission of crimes, organizational structure, the use of symbols and rituals (such as initiation rites), a code of honor, and a specific type of language and communicative system used tactically among members (called *cants* or simply distinctive criminal slangs). The moniker is key for establishing identity and connecting the criminal organization to a specific geographical locale, much like the surname of people does – hence, for instance, Yakuza (Japan), Triads (China), Cosa Nostra (Italy), Hells Angels (United States), and so on.

The term *mafia* (as discussed in the Introduction) is often misused to refer to organized criminal groups in general – Albanian Mafia, Bulgarian Mafia, and so on. This term was used initially to identify a specific organized crime group that was founded and still operates in Sicily, Italy. Perhaps, because the Sicilian Mafia is among the most well-known crime syndicates and has received enormous attention from the media and Hollywood, the term *mafia* has erroneously become a synonym for organized crime. Given the advent of the Internet and the consequences that this entails for everyone, including organized crime, we will refer retroactively to organized crime that took root in real territorial space as "Mafia 1.0." The term also alludes to the fact that mafia-type organizations used the technologies that emerged in the Web 1.0 society – essentially a telecommunications world without current social media platforms. So the term "Mafia 1.0" is used here in reference to both the "real world mafias" before the advent of cyberspace and as denizens of Web 1.0 society after its arrival.

All Mafia and Mafia-like criminal organizations trace their roots to some founding myth, such as medieval knights, ninja warriors, sacred monks, and the like. The stories they tell about themselves reflect what has been called the "Robin Hood principle" (Hobsbawm, 1959, Seal, 2009, Nicaso and Danesi, 2021), whereby traditional organized crime is purported to have risen from among ordinary people, usually in the medieval era, to rob the rich so as to help the poor, with noble warriors fighting against oppression and corrupt governments. To remain united, the "noble bandits" subsequently developed a self-styled micro-social system based on internal organization, with a leader and subalterns, symbols for decorating acts of bravery, initiation rituals, codes of conduct, and recruitment procedures. By the late nineteenth century, the noble warriors became increasingly more organized and well connected to the authorities of their countries, entering into a corruption-based system of collaboration with them, thus ensuring their continuity and sustained recruitment. Without a Robin Hood origin story, however, they would never have gained a foothold in their social milieus. Made-up histories repeatedly become real and are thus almost impossible to differentiate from accurate historiographical accounts. As such, they are opportunistic self-constructive strategies, tapping into dire social conditions that render people susceptible to manipulation.

In the case of the Mafia, for instance, Sicily's history of economic underdevelopment led to the rise of secret criminal societies (*compagnie d'armi*), initially employed by the ruling classes to protect their privileges. It was born, more specifically, during the transition period from the Bourbon regime to a liberal state, when mobsters aligned themselves to resistance movements, gaining legitimacy and social status. The violence of the reaction-resistance groups (which eventually became the mafia) was different from that of bandits, pirates, and brigands who openly challenged the established power figures and structures. Strategic violence allowed the mobsters to use threats and to wield "silent influence" over victims due to forging corrupt relationships with the immoral ruling classes. From this social milieu, mafia-type organizations eventually arose, not as liberators of the oppressed but as scheming individuals intent on obtaining their share of wealth and privilege however they could.

The main activities of the Mafia 1.0 have always revolved around extortion and influence peddling, using the threat of physical retribution for noncompliance as a central operational strategy, which remains the main form of fear-based control over people. Given their internal organizational stability and use of strategic violence, traditional organized crime groupings became little fiefdoms of their own, able to remain united because of their commitment to secrecy and punishment codes, should any member dare to engage in any act of betrayal. Moreover, they were largely able to neutralize the capability of police forces to do anything about them, given the self-serving political affiliations that the mobsters forged between themselves and the authorities, including members of the police. The same dynamics and pattern of operation were found across the ocean in America. In 1915, the Chicago City Council Committee on Crime noted, revealingly, that the power of the criminal groups lay in their ability to

> escape from detection, by collusion or connivance, or incompetence of the police, by the work of the professional fixer; by the pressure of political influence; by the inactivity and incompetence of prosecutors; the spineless attitude of some judges, or by some loophole of escape in the mazes of criminal law.
> *(Merriam, 1915: 164)*

While money is essential to the operations of traditional organized crime, and is obtained with violence and fear tactics, their ultimate goal is power, not money in itself but rather in its ability to bestow clout and self-serving authority upon them. Mafia-type organizations have always seen themselves as independent or parallel nation-states with their own military, rules of conduct, and ethical norms, seeking to exercise control over people, territories, and institutions. They have no sense of *mens rea*, or the consciousness of doing something criminal, seeing their illegal operations instead as part of their business plan or agenda. Honor is also a major factor in the construction of their pseudo-moral codes. The violence used by mobsters has a specific strategic objective – to settle debts, back up their protection rackets, intimidate victims and corrupt officials, settle disputes among members, defer competition, control the workforce, manage labor relations, enforce contract and verbal agreements, and punish members for acting illegally outside of prescribed criminal operations. Typically, sometimes, the violence is more psychological than it is physical.

The term *mafia* was permanently ensconced into American group-think during the hearings of the Permanent Subcommittee of the Senate Committee on Operations, chaired by Senator Estes Kefauver, from May 1950 to May 1951. The Committee was the first to connect organized crime to popular culture, pointing out that

> Through the medium of television, the citizens of the country for the first time had it driven home to them with dramatic and startling impact that top-ranking hoodlums and underworld leaders were in their midst and were not story-book characters.
> *(Kefauver, 1951)*

It can be claimed, as Kefauver suggested, that without the media, organized crime would have largely retreated to the dark corners of society, remaining anonymous. Movies such as *Scarface*, *The Godfather*, and *Goodfellas*, and television programs such as *The Sopranos*, normalized the American Cosa Nostra in the public eye, despite its brutal activities. It is interesting to note that in Italy, it was not until 1982 that the parliament passed its first anti-Mafia legislation with provisions for the seizure and confiscation of criminal gains. Before that, the Italian Criminal Code contained reference only to an "unlawful association" whose purpose was to commit crimes – a legal notion that goes back to the 1588 Papal Bull of Pope Sixtus V, which defined crime as an act of association, for the first time, as a way to counteract the rise of the Huguenots – a French Protestant group who suffered persecution at the hands of the Catholic papacies. Eventually, the Napoleonic Code came into force, with its stress on clearly written and accessible law, replacing the previous patchwork of laws, leading over time to labeling criminal gangs as outlaws.

As mentioned, a central goal of traditional mafias was to create and maintain a self-styled autonomous parallel culture to the mainstream one in which they existed socially and geographically, assigning an ersatz legitimacy and historical mystique unto themselves. As Lunde (2004: 11) has emphasized, "Successful organized crime groups each have their own mystique, ensuring solidarity and loyalty through shared ethnicity, kinship, or allegiance to a code of behavior." As such, the Mafia 1.0 became normalized as a covert parallel culture in society, interacting with the overt culture whenever it was deemed necessary or advantageous. For instance, before the introduction of stricter laws by the government, including those targeting businesses with links to the organization, the Japanese Yakuza had inserted themselves into mainstream Japanese culture and society, operating legitimate businesses and engaging directly with the political system. Similar stories can be told about most of traditional organized crime syndicates. A large part of their staying power is that they have remained separate from, yet connected to, mainstream society, carrying out their corrosive activities virtually without notice. They are a sort of "enemy within," as the former General Prosecutor of Palermo, Sicily, Roberto Scarpinato (2015: 129), described Cosa Nostra, the Sicilian Mafia: "The evil we are fighting out of us is also among us, inside us." With the migration to cyberspace, the "enemy within" has become even more undetectable, making him enormously more dangerous.

The land-based mafias organized themselves in various ways related to territorial factors (Catino, 2019). The diagram in Figure 1.1, which provides a model of abstract organizational structure, can be applied generically to most of different traditional organized crime groups.

In all mafia-type organizations, there is a boss or leader, assisted by an accountant who shares a complementary leadership function to the operation of the criminal group. Below are regents, group heads, area managers, and affiliates. The same hierarchical structure has been transposed to online cyber-criminal groups, but it has been expanded considerably and revalued operationally. For example, programmers, IT experts, and hackers, among others with computer skills, are adjunct members within this structure, operating mainly apart from the traditional mafia hierarchy while interacting with members at different levels of operation. The real-world activities of trafficking and physical violence are, however, still part of the mafias' activities in real space and cyberspace. The main difference between the Mafia 1.0 and the current mafias (Mafia 2.0) is that the Web 2.0 world offers new

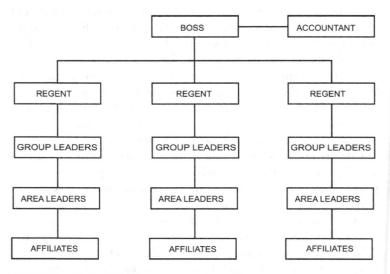

FIGURE 1.1 Mafia 1.0 Organizational Structure

criminal opportunities to them, providing a virtual locus for planning real-world crimes with other criminal organizations, no matter who they are or where they operate geographically.

Mafia 2.0: Migration to Cyberspace

The migration to cyberspace on the part of mafia-type organizations can be conflated into the moniker of "Mafia 2.0," as mentioned. This does not imply in any way that the physical-world mafias have disappeared or substituted in their entirety by cyber mafias. On the contrary, the two now form a continuum, with one dimension (organized crime in hyperreality) complementing and reinforcing the other (organized crime in reality). On this continuum, locating any boundary point is difficult if not impossible. This may well be a direct effect of living in the world of the matrix, where the blurring of the lines between the two dimensions has crystallized into a *simulacrum effect*. This psychological mechanism blends the two into one overall mental outlook, as Baudrillard (1981) claimed. So in the realm of the Mafia 2.0, crimes committed in cyberspace and those in real space are no longer seen as qualitatively different but as continuous forms of criminality – a state of mind that results from the simulacrum effect. The same effect also may be seen as the cause of the dualistic character that the Mafia 2.0 has developed (to be discussed subsequently). In no other era would such a lack of distinction have been thinkable.

In 2018, Europol (the European Union Agency for Law Enforcement Cooperation) defined cybercrimes as "traditional crimes facilitated by the Internet," such as extortion, theft, fraud, and intimidation, aided in new ways by the Internet and digital technologies. Organized criminal groups do not use the ordinary (surface) Internet to conduct their illegal activities; they use its so-called "dark regions," to be discussed in detail in Chapter 3. Suffice it to say here that these are the inaccessible parts of the Internet, called the Dark Web, which are overlay networks that use the Internet but require specific software and authorization to gain access. These networks allow businesses and individuals to carry out their affairs anonymously without divulging identifying information, such as a user's location. Dark Web technologies thus enable criminals to plan their crimes in cyberspace and engage in new kinds of crimes made possible by Dark Web locales. They are virtual sites where the different mafias of the world can come together to plan their operations, irrespective of their traditional distinctiveness. Cyberspace has made transnational organized crime a dark reality (literally).

The Mafia 1.0 lived in the "upperworld" of real space; the Mafia 2.0 inhabits the "underworld" of the Dark Web. The anonymity and inter-cooperation among criminal organizations and even terrorists that this region of cyberspace defines organized crime, allowing it to refashion and expand its operations since the turn of the Millennium. For the first time in the history of mafias, crimes can be more easily planned and committed through collaborative efforts of different criminals regardless of their national borders – in fact, crimes that are planned by one criminal organization in one state might be carried out in another. Even collaboration between criminal organizations and terrorist groups has become commonplace, as is evident in the trafficking of illicit drugs – which has led to the spread of *narco-terrorism*, describing a relationship whereby terrorist groups, criminal organizations, and drug cartels work in a broader type of partnership that could have come about only in cyberspace. The drug trade itself is controlled by criminal cartels, which are allowed to operate by terrorist groups in some countries, such as Colombia and Afghanistan, given that a considerable financial share of the earnings from drug cartels is then given to terrorists, allowing them to carry out their political agendas better, influencing local and national politics (D'Alfonso, 2014). Criminal organizations and political terrorists may have different motives, but they are not averse to opportunistic cooperation. Mafia 2.0 organizations have become sophisticated and multinational, capable of engaging with criminality worldwide. They have entered the global village seamlessly and surreptitiously to carry out their business relatively risk-free, making immense profits. Organized crime has thus gone from localized, national enterprises to global, multinational ones. Along the way, criminal organizations have adapted to changing market forces and political climates, showing themselves as adaptive, clever entrepreneurs. Drugs remain a staple for cyber-criminal groups, but land swindles, tax frauds, online gambling, social engineering scams, phishing schemes, and the like are now major money-making activities. However, in the global village, there are new risks that mafias face, including the possibility of police forces interrupting their cyber-criminal operations with new powerful cyber tools themselves. Italian sociologist Letizia Paoli (2003) has suggested that the main risk is, actually, the loss of traditional identities as distinctive self-contained cultures, given that the historical *raison d'être* of mafia-type organizations has always been predicated on the maintenance of such identities, keeping them averse to any merger with other criminal groups, which would have been seen as counterproductive. So as Paoli intimates, a paradigm shift in the identity-constitutive nature of criminal cultures has been underway in cyberspace since the turn of the Millennium – a topic that has enormous implications for the future of organized crime (to be discussed subsequently).

As mentioned, migration to cyberspace has brought about the need for new operational structures and roles, incorporated into the established organizational templates of the different mafias (Winder, 2017). The general structure of cyber gang organization can be shown in Figure 1.2.

As can be seen, there is still a leader, but in this case, the leader possesses considerable technical skills, which certainly was not always the case of the bosses of the traditional mafias. But the boss figure has not been eliminated; instead, he now works alongside the team leader, who has the requisite tech savvy to ensure the organization's smooth operation. Right below is the coder, who is an expert in computer programming and knowledgeable of trends in software technologies and hence able to develop appropriate criminal malware. Below are

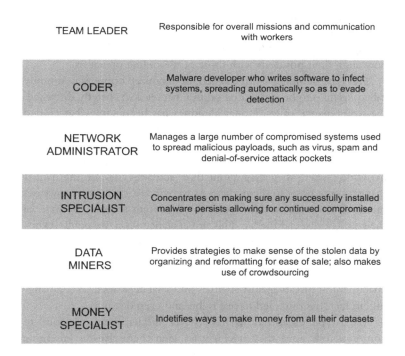

TEAM LEADER	Responsible for overall missions and communication with workers
CODER	Malware developer who writes software to infect systems, spreading automatically so as to evade detection
NETWORK ADMINISTRATOR	Manages a large number of compromised systems used to spread malicious payloads, such as virus, spam and denial-of-service attack pockets
INTRUSION SPECIALIST	Concentrates on making sure any successfully installed malware persists allowing for continued compromise
DATA MINERS	Provides strategies to make sense of the stolen data by organizing and reformatting for ease of sale; also makes use of crowdsourcing
MONEY SPECIALIST	Indetifies ways to make money from all their datasets

FIGURE 1.2   Cybercriminal Organization

the administrator, intrusion specialist, and data miners, who manage the technology in various ways. Finally, there is the money specialist who determines how best to make money from the datasets the system has illegally acquired. Online gangs also use standard social media platforms like WhatsApp, Slack, and Telegram to conduct parts of their business in real time, which do not require concealment, in addition to the hidden tools that exist only on the Dark Web. There is, moreover, a two-dimensional division of roles, with some assigned to the online dimension of operations and the other to the offline dimension. These dimensions are however in a state of constant fusion, which will be shaped by changing technologies (as will be discussed subsequently). In effect, mafia-type organizations have not abandoned their offline (real world) activities. On the contrary, the two are seen as related and continuous. Some of these – for example, drug trafficking – involve coordination of the two dimensions, whereby particular individuals or groups in the real world carry out online planning among several criminal organizations. Moreover, in the overall structure of mafia-type organizations, the roles of *capo (Boss)*, lieutenants, and foot soldiers remain in place largely. But they now align their positions with those of the online operators. This type of online–offline system of organized crime is commonly called *hybrid* – to be elaborated on in Chapter 2. As briefly discussed, the maintenance of traditional identities has been somewhat eroded because the young bosses do not desire to remain anonymous. They literally come out of the shadows to post their photos, profiles, and messages on Facebook, Instagram, TikTok, and other social media networks, where they brag about their activities, despite the danger that exposure poses to themselves. As we will see, there are many cases in which investigators have been able to locate fugitives because of their posts on social media. This nonchalance vis-à-vis public exposure constitutes a paradigm shift in mafia culture and psychology. In the United States and Canada, it is called cyber-banging, which refers to displaying criminal power, the recruitment of members, and the enactment of threats against enemies on social networks. Cyber-banging, in fact, has often led to real fights and even death.

Mafia-type organizations have never hidden their presence to common folk since they have always seen themselves as emerging from them. But they kept their existence low key. This no longer holds. While Mafia 1.0 members did aim to convey a certain appearance in public that set them somewhat apart, including tattoos and specific types of dress, they also wanted to convey a dignified personality, keeping a low profile – a behavior that bears little or no meaning today to the young *capi*. Significantly, Twitter accounts of alleged Mexican drug traffickers have attracted the attention of the international media on the lifestyles of the so-called "narco-juniors," second generation of drug traffickers that have inherited the leadership of large criminal organizations.

The split character of the Mafia 2.0 – its hybrid format and its utilization of the visible Internet for reasons of braggadocio – is the essence of what will be called "cool mafia" in this book. Like anyone else living in the matrix age, the new generations of mafiosi spend a lot of time on the Internet where they have developed a form of psychological addiction. But even this has its own set of advantages. As Weimann (2006) has argued and illustrated, the Internet allows for accessible communication among members, an increased facility in sharing information on operations (in a coded way), the use of

training videos for members and recruits, a system to research potential targets, and a locus for recruitment pitches for new membership.
This is a "nuanced agenda," as Weimann suggests, that plays on the
desire for visible empowerment felt by many young mafiosi – a pattern that an examination of their social media sites corroborates (discussed subsequently).

Cybercriminality

The question of why organized crime exists in the first place and
why, to this day, many young people desire to join them has been the
subject of a host of theories in criminology, psychology, sociology,
anthropology, and other social sciences. Among the various factors
that criminologists have identified as motivators the following stand
out:

- *Differential Association*: this claims that criminal behavior is learned
  by those young people who want to imitate it, aiming to become
  part of the criminal organization they admire. Among the factors involved are the influence of glorified criminal lifestyles,
  the desire to escape from poverty, and upbringing in a criminal
  environment.
- *Differential Opportunity*: this claims that when there is a dis-
  crepancy between societal expectations for success and limited
  opportunities to pursue them, the resulting tension induces some
  young people to seek the expected success in gangs and criminal
  organizations in general.
- *Social Control*: this claims that when there are inadequate social
  controls or constraints, some young people may take advantage of
  the situation by engaging in criminal activities, which they might
  perceive as enhancing their personal image and boosting financial
  possibilities.
- *Anomie*: this explains criminality in terms of a lack or diminishment of ethical norms or values in a rearing situation – a situation
  that might lead some young people to seek in criminal organizations the missing norms or values.
- *Subculture Theory*: this claims that some young (typically rebel-
  lious) people are attracted to criminal subcultures because they
  allow them to set themselves apart from the social and cultural
  mainstream.

- *Ethnic Succession*: this maintains that criminal gangs in immigrant communities often arise to help young people achieve economic parity with the dominant classes.
- *Psychoanalysis*: this focuses on the effects of upbringing factors, such as the repression of impulses, that potentially induce some young people to seek a criminal lifestyle to satisfy them.
- *Rational Choice*: this claims that the decision to join criminal groups is made by young people themselves as a matter of choice, not of necessity, by weighing the costs and benefits of their decision.
- *Underclass Theory*: this claims that involvement in crime is a natural response to the harsh influence of street life associated with impoverished populations living in both urban and suburban areas.
- *Egoistic altruism*: this claims that joining a criminal group is motivated by self-interest, since it is seen as providing a means to enhance one's own sense of worth and as a way to increase one's control over the social environment of one's upbringing. There is in such cases a kind of reciprocal motivation – "you scratch my back and I scratch yours"

Another motivational factor is that some young people find organized crime exciting in itself, a form of escape from boredom and routine – a factor that Mexican cartels seem to have understood today, taking advantage of the new ways of escape offered by social media and other digital systems. An example is in the domain of role-playing videogames (RPGs). These powerful forms of virtual interaction produce the simulacrum effect, thus making it psychologically easy for users to move from the fantasy world into the real world of cybercriminality, guided there by clever criminals. As Gary Fine (1983: 59–60) observed already in the early 1980s, for many players, RPGs constitute an essential aspect of daily life, providing "a structure for making friends and finding a sense of community," as well as allowing players to "endow themselves with attributes that in reality, they do not possess: strength, social poise, rugged good looks, wisdom, and chivalric skills." As Taylor (2006) has also argued, RPGs serve a socializing function, providing a tribal-like locus as a place to engage with others. The studies collected by Adams and Smith (2008) showed, in fact, that RPGs offer numerous possibilities for people who share common interests and fantasies to engage in them collectively as if they were in "electronic tribes." It is a small step from the electronic tribe to the real criminal one. Our perusal of social media posts of various organized criminal groups has shown, in fact, that videogame culture is both attractive to the criminals themselves and a means for them to reach out to young people, enticing them to become part of a criminal organization. In effect, online videogames seem to provide an easy access point into the lives of young people, allowing criminals to strike up a conversation and then build trust (discussed subsequently). As Dalby (2021) has noted concerning the recruitment of young people by the Mexican drug cartels:

> This fits a pattern reported by numerous young gamers in Mexico in recent months. Messages are sent in the early hours of the morning, when parents are unlikely to be supervising their children's online activity, openly inviting young gamers to join criminal groups and selling this as a glamorous lifestyle. Some messages alleged that they were being sent by the Sinaloa Cartel or the Jalisco Cartel New Generation . . . after contacting young people online, the representatives of criminal groups invite them to in-person meetings where they are abducted and forced to join.

The point here is that in addition to the traditional theories of organized crime, concepts such as the simulacrum effect must be taken into account in any consideration of the factors motivating young people in joining gangs in the era of the Internet (McCaffree and Proctor, 2018). It should be stressed, however, that the research has not shown any direct correlation between RPGs and real-world violence; our point is simply that they are used by drug cartel members both as recreation for themselves and as entry points into young people's minds. It's also a way to take advantage of the simulacrum effect, incentivizing young people to become members of a criminal organization, casting a positive light on those who possess hacking skills. Cybercrime began with young hackers who defaced websites or erased data for mischief and self-enjoyment. But soon, the underworld of criminal organizations started hiring these hackers, as they once hired hitmen and enforcers. Police takedowns of Mexican drug cartels have shown that they consist of kidnapped IT engineers and specialists, who had been forced to work for the cartels.

In summary, two criminal cultures have developed in tandem – the traditional real world and the digital virtual one, evolving in parallel. The hybrid Mafia 2.0 world shows that organized criminal groups are ever-evolving entities, even if this means breaking away in some part from behaviors and values of the past. There could be cyber-mafiosi from anywhere and from all social classes, nations, and ethnicities. The *capi* have also adapted – they are increasingly digital natives who are comfortable with the new technologies and understand the advantages offered by cybercriminality. The Al Capone wise guy may still have a symbolic presence in organized crime, but he is ceding more and more to the sophisticated tech-savvy leader who can victimize people both in the real world and on the Internet.

The merging of real and virtual worlds, with one affecting the other, is now a fact of criminal life, as evidenced by recurring stories, such as the one of Fabio Orefici, an alleged member of Mele clan of Pianura, a district of Naples. He was wounded on October 16, 2014, in an ambush. From the hospital, he posted a photo on Facebook that showed him with a bandage under his left shoulder and a message announcing his revenge: "the lion is wounded, but he is not dead. I am already up. Open your eyes well; it doesn't take anything to close them. Avita murrii (You have to die)." Four days later, his front door was broached by a blast of machine guns in response to the message he had launched through Facebook.

However, there is a paradox here, as Paoli (2003) pointed out at the beginning of organized cybercriminality – even though mafia-type organizations are adaptive, they are also steeped in traditions, which have been the primary stabilizing factors that have kept them cohesive. But these very traditions may be on the wane, indicating that the very concept of a "mafia" culture is evolving adaptively, leaving previous established practices of organized crime behind. Nonetheless, as she also stresses, traditional hierarchical style of organization, especially in the centralization of power, continues to guide operations and differentiation of roles. In effect, cyberspace has brought about significant changes to how traditions and patterns of interaction are perceived in the world of organized crime. In the pre-Internet world, criminal organizations could fix the boundaries of their operations; in cyberspace, this is no longer true, a fact that has had repercussions for organized crime in general, as the two worlds (the real and the hyper-real) have formed a merger (Jaishankar, 2011, Maras, 2016, Leukfeldt and Holt, 2019). As documented by the United Nations Office on

Drugs and Crime (2019), this merger has led to a three-part classification of organized crime.

- Type I: groups that predominantly operate online, committing cybercrimes; they are divided into *swarms* (relatively less structured) and *hubs* (relatively more structured).
- Type II: groups that carry out offline and online criminal activities in a coordinated fashion; they are further classified into *clustered hybrids* (small groups that cluster around the commission of specific cybercrimes) and *extended hybrids* (highly complex groups operating offline and online).
- Type III: groups that utilize online technology to facilitate offline crimes; they are subdivided into *hierarchies* (traditional organized criminal groups that use technology routinely) and *aggregates* (transient groups that use the Internet for limited reasons).

Following up on Paoli's observation, the question becomes: Has this merger affected the age-old sense of distinctive identity to which mafia-type organizations have held on tenaciously? Does it make sense any longer to identify mafias with the old monikers, such as Yakuza, Triads, or Camorra? Has there been a hybridization of identity? Such questions will be addressed throughout the remaining of this book. The definition of organized crime by the United Nations Convention as existing in some location for a while is clearly in need of revision, since, in cyberspace, the geographic location is vague at best, and, in some cases, even nonexistent.

One way to portray organized cybercriminality is in terms of three intersecting dimensions – human, behavioral, and simulative – as argued cogently by Maalem Lahcen et al. (2020). These can be represented as shown in Figure 1.3.

In this model, the term "dirty dozen" refers to the twelve most common types of cybercrimes (phishing, social engineering, hacking, and so on) and MARC to a computer-related mailing list archive – MARC stands for "Machine-Readable Cataloging," in reference to define a format that allows for rapid classification of data. While this model was intended for investigators, it can easily be applied to the psychology of organized cybercrime itself, which involves a blend of the same type of human, behavioral, and simulative factors. The latter aspect – called the simulacrum effect here – is the one we have stressed, since, in our view, it differentiates organized crime today from all previous forms.

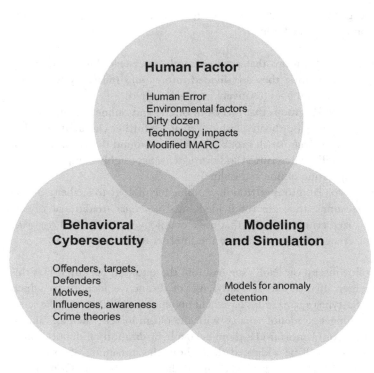

FIGURE 1.3 Cybercriminality

In a nutshell, this refers to the effect of new technologies on shaping cognition, behaviors, and modes of communication.

Case Studies: I

The case studies for this chapter are well-known; they are discussed here to show how Mafia 2.0 now operates and what police agencies use to combat the new forms of organized crime. They are intended to provide a historical snapshot of organized crime as it has moved from real space to cyberspace, showing how this has changed its character from a land-based one to a hybrid one. Like everyone else who lives in the world of the matrix, the Mafia 2.0 has understood that the real and the hyperreal are now inseparable, with one influencing the other. These case studies constitute our initial attempt to illustrate what is required to answer the overall question we intend to address in this book: What has happened to mafia-type organizations in the global village?

Case Study: ShadowCrew

ShadowCrew was a website considered to be the forerunner of today's cybercrime forums. It operated from August 2002 to November 2004, facilitating the sale of drugs and providing information on hacking techniques, social engineering strategies, credit card fraud schemes, and phishing operations. U.S. federal agents brought the site down after arresting one of its founders, Johnny Cumba, who became an informant and provided information allowing agents to monitor the site and its users. The federal indictment stated that "Shadowcrew was an international organization of approximately 4,000 members" (United States District Court of New Jersey Indictment, SSC/2003R01260). The website is a point-of-departure for documenting the history of hybrid organized crime. In 2019, CNN acknowledged this by releasing the documentary, *Declassified: Untold Stories of American Spies*, which told of the Secret Service's investigation into ShadowCrew.

The documentary emphasized that ShadowCrew was a pivotal moment for the rise and spread of cybercriminality, showing how various roles and levels of criminal operations could be easily managed by computer programmers, intrusion specialists, data miners, hackers, and others. ShadowCrew's organization spread broadly right after, leading to the emergence of the Mafia 2.0:

- At the top of the chain of command were the "administrators" who maintained the website and dictated who could become members.
- Next in line were the "moderators" who oversaw and monitored the discussion forums and posts, establishing participation rules.
- Then came the "reviewers," who managed the illicit services and merchandise distribution, including counterfeit passports and stolen credit cards.
- Finally, there were the general members who participated in forums sharing tips about cybercrime and buying the illicit services and goods. ShadowCrew membership was exclusive and operated on the basis of avowed loyalty, akin to traditional organized crime.

• Overall, it was a loose global network of individuals seeking financial benefit. Members used nicknames to maintain anonymity and were prohibited from sharing personal information.

Significantly, the website adopted traditional notions of organized crime, including a hierarchization of roles, rules for members, and the implementation of secrecy. A key attraction of the site for subsequent criminal organizations was that it could operate without the need for physical violence or physical control over geographical territories. ShadowCrew also made it evident that law enforcement had to adapt technologically to take it down successfully.

Case Study: Silk Road

Silk Road was the first modern dark marketplace – a part of Dark Web that allowed users to browse it anonymously, without fear of traffic monitoring. The website was launched in February 2011, offering illicit goods and services to over 100,000 buyers. In October 2013, the FBI shut down the website, arresting Ross Ulbricht, the site's founder. However, this did not stop the site from continuing. A month later, in November 2013, Silk Road 2.0 came online, run by former administrators. This, too, was eventually shut down a year later, in November 2014, as part of Operation Onymous. Ulbricht was convicted of seven charges in a Federal Court in Manhattan and sentenced to life in prison (United States of America v. Ross William Ulbricht, 14-cr-68 KBF). In November 2020, the United States government seized over one billion dollars' worth of bitcoin connected to Silk Road.

As the first Dark Web criminal operation, Silk Road has become a point of reference in all subsequent studies of, and connections to, the Dark Mafia. It also became a prototype for hybrid cybercriminality ever since, characterized by: (1) the leadership of tech-savvy hackers and programmers; (2) the use of cryptocurrency because it is virtually untraceable; and (3) the employment of a "money mule," an individual recruited to transfer goods between parties and launder the money exchanged (Maras, 2016). Drug trafficking could thus be planned online but realized through role players like money mules or by enlisting the cooperation of hired criminals in specific geographic locations, which are amenable to criminal operations. So, a city like Montreal has often been chosen as a drug trafficking site due to its ideal location. It has a large port of entry situated on the Saint

Lawrence Seaway and is close to the New York state border. Drugs can be imported and exported quite easily to the United States by the money mules. At the border, drug traffickers use various methods to get across, including bribing officials, using boats in the summer in a clandestine manner, or driving across on skidoos in the winter (Revels and Cummings, 2014).

The importance of money mules was brought out by a 2018 case in which an anonymous criminal group was involved in conducting a business email compromise attack, duping targets into transferring money by wire, masquerading as legitimate partners with whom the business had worked previously. Money mules would then use wire transfers and open up bank accounts for shell companies, keeping a portion of the money deposited into the accounts, transferred to a bank in Poland or China. The FBI eventually brought down the scam under the aegis of Operation Wire Wire (2018). Agents executed search warrants and issued warning letters. Fifteen money mules were eventually charged for their roles in defrauding victims. In a way, they represent the new foot soldiers of organized cybercrime. But unlike the traditional foot soldiers, their employment is transient, changing on a job-to-job basis.

Case Study: Operation Trojan Horse Shield

An example of how police forces now engage with cyber-criminals is the sting operation known as Trojan Horse Shield, involving the FBI, the U.S. Drug Enforcement Administration, the Dutch National Police, the Australian Federal Police, the Swedish Police Authority (Polisen), and Europol. The operation involved the creation of a smartphone app called Anom, which allowed the authorities to gain access to over 10,000 encrypted devices of over 300 criminal syndicates operating in over 100 countries, utilizing technologies such as remote wipes and duress passwords. Between 2018 and 2021, the operation intercepted millions of messages sent through Anom, enabling police agencies to monitor the criminal communications. This resulted in the arrest of over 800 suspects in 16 countries. Among the arrested were alleged members of the Australian-based 'Ndrangheta, Albanian crime gangs, outlaw motorcycle clubs, drug cartels, and other criminal organizations. Notably, it led to the arrest of an elusive fugitive 'Ndrangheta boss named Rocco Morabito, who had escaped to Brazil from a jail in Uruguay, awaiting extradition to Italy to complete his 30-year prison term for drug trafficking.

The importance of Anom was stated explicitly in United States District Court for the Southern District of California (Case '21 MJO1948, p. 8), which is worth repeating here because it summarizes how technology and transnational cooperation among police agencies now characterize investigations:

> The FBI opened a new covert investigation, Operation Trojan Shield, which centered on exploiting Anom by inserting it into criminal networks and working with international partners, including the Australian Federal Police ("AFP"), to monitor the communications. Before the device could be put to use, however, the FBI, AFP, and the CHS (Confidential Human Sources) built a master key into the existing encryption system which surreptitiously attaches to each message and enables law enforcement to decrypt and store the message as it is transmitted. A user of Anom is unaware of this capability. By design, as part of the Trojan Shield investigation, for devices located outside of the United States, an encrypted "BCC" of the message is routed to an "iBot" server located outside of the United States, where it is decrypted from the CHS's encryption code and then immediately re-encrypted with FBI encryption code. The newly encrypted message then passes to a second FBI-owned iBot server, where it is decrypted and its content available for viewing in the first instance.

The point is that as organized crime has changed, so too has law enforcement. This is not a moot point, given that mafia-type organizations have always eluded the law, able to guarantee their continuity via many clever evasive strategies. In cyberspace, it may be easier to bring them down, with ingenious strategies such as the Trojan Horse Shield. Of course, criminals are nothing if not adaptive and clever, as they coopt new technologies to enhance their operational base and to avoid detection (Chapter 5).

Case Study: Coronavirus Scams

In 2020, during the height of the coronavirus pandemic, lockdowns were imposed throughout the world. This situation gave organized crime a unique opportunity for profiteering, allowing them to get drugs to the streets, away from police scrutiny, via online sales and courier deliveries. In some countries, gangs used unwitting drivers working for essential services to provide door-to-door deliveries. Despite social distancing, closures, and other measures to limit the spread of the coronavirus, the drug trade picked up considerably. Police seizures in March and April 2020 showed that tons of drugs were being moved around easily, even as land borders had become more strictly supervised.

According to the authorities we talked to (see Acknowledgments), activities were typically planned through encrypted online techniques. In some cases, hackers impersonated reliable organizations, such as the World Health Organization, allowing them to spread their malware extensively. As a result, the number of online operations during the pandemic spiraled, as criminal organizations used such activities as phishing scams, duping many to provide personal information that was used for fraudulent purposes, and offering fake coronavirus tests and treatments. The World Customs Organization estimated that such fraudulent activity was worth about 7 percent of world trade. Law enforcement agencies found over 2,000 online links advertising items related to the pandemic. Of these, counterfeit surgical masks were the most commonly sold online. As a result of such widespread criminal activities, an Interpol Operation, dubbed *Pangea*, in which 90 countries took part, was established as part of a collective police action against the illicit online sale of medicines and medical products.

The cybercriminal groups clearly saw the pandemic as an opportunity to exploit human needs, weakness, and gullibility. Media reports in Italy, throughout the pandemic, confirmed that Mafia, 'Ndrangheta, and Camorra were highly active, even reemerging in parts of Sicily and Campania as Robin Hood figures, distributing food to the poorer neighborhoods. Similar stories were echoed in many regions, from Latin America to Japan. The most interesting one occurred in Mexico, where the daughter of a well-known drug trafficker had sent parcels containing necessities of life marked with a stylized photo of her father.

The operations during the pandemic reflected an old tactic, aiming to increase the mafias' status and credibility in a region and step in as an alternative to the incompetent legal state. Virginia Comolli (2021) aptly summarizes the event as follows:

> Organized criminal networks are known for their adaptability and the rapidity with which they exploit opportunities. The

introduction of quarantine measures has impacted licit and illicit businesses alike, and restrictions of movement have prompted a doubling of efforts into cybercrime, fraud and counterfeiting whilst many forms of physical crime have momentarily slowed down. Furthermore, the COVID-19 pandemic has created opportunities for both organized criminal organizations and less sophisticated gangs in countries as diverse as, for instance, Brazil, Italy, Japan and South Africa to impose or expand their informal control and governance systems in the affected areas by distributing supplies and helping local communities during lockdowns. That "help" comes with strings attached. In the post-pandemic period, it is reasonable to expect that criminals will take advantage of, among others, the expected economic downturn, growing unemployment levels, new opportunities for smuggling economic migrants, and changes in consumer demands and practices.

The 2020 report of the Global Initiative Against Transnational Organized Crime remarked that the pandemic greatly enhanced organized criminal operations, including smuggling, human and drug trafficking, robberies, and burglaries, as it reflected at the same time a decrease in other kinds of organized criminal activities. As the report noted, determining the confines of criminal operations today is impossible, given the global reach of the Internet and the new criminal opportunities it makes available to criminals.

Case Study: Operation Fontana-Almabahía

In 2021, a criminal organization operating out of Santa Cruz de Tenerife was dismantled by the Spanish Police in collaboration with the Italian Postal and Communications Police Service. The operation, called Fontana-Almabahía, was coordinated by the Public Prosecutor's Office of Bari and the Spanish judiciary, assisted by Eurojust and Europol. The group was an Italian criminal association based in Tenerife, from where it was carrying out online fraud and money laundering. The investigators reconstructed the entire pyramidal structure of the criminal organization, which used hackers specialized in phishing and vishing (voice phishing using telephones) to coordinate the attacks. The criminal organization used the latest-generation computer tools and social engineering techniques, managing to take possession of the bank codes of Italian victims, and then transferring the pilfered money into Spanish current accounts through money mules, also of Italian nationality, who had been recruited in Spain. The sums stolen were then laundered through the purchase of cryptocurrency or reinvested in other criminal activities, such as prostitution, drug trafficking, and arms trafficking, for a turnover of over ten million euros. This case showed, above all else, that criminal operations can now sprout up almost anywhere spontaneously via cyberspace. It also showed how a new and powerful form of psychological crime, known as social engineering, had become intrinsic to cybercriminality. This is the manipulation of people into performing actions or divulging confidential information. It differs from the traditional "con" because it is one of the various steps in a more complex fraud scheme. An improperly secured password-recovery system grants a malicious attacker full access to a user's account while the original user will lose access to it. This case study will be discussed in more detail in Chapter 2.

Case Study: An Online Italian Betting Operation

A five-billion-euro online gaming operation was brought down on January 11, 2022, with 33 arrests (in Italy and abroad), 11 websites seized, and two companies – Europartner and Iocosa Ludum cooperative – dismantled, as a result of the activities of the Carabinieri of Salerno. The head of the gaming operation was Luigi Giuseppe Cirillo, son of the late boss, Giuseppe Cirillo, originally from Campania, who had moved to Northern Calabria in the 1970s. According to the investigators, he had created a holding company involved in online gaming, the DGB Poker network, not authorized in Italy, offering live dealer games, in-play betting, mobile poker, roulette, and sportsbook betting. Among the crimes alleged against Cirillo were money laundering in tax havens, such as Panama, and using the proceeds of his criminal activities to buy real estate. Interestingly, the investigators also discovered a luxurious Lamborghini Murcielago, registered to a fake company in the Czech Republic, which would have been sold to a dealership in Turin and the money deposited into a Panama bank under the name of Cirillo. Cirillo's platform was linked to the Casalesi clan – a clan within the Camorra, operating from Casal di Principe and San Cipriano d'Aversa in the province of Caserta, between Naples and Latium. It is believed to be one of the most powerful groups within the Camorra, and Cirillo's plan was seemingly to forge a partnership with them via his online operation. The Carabinieri, supported by the police forces in Panama (and other places), cooperated in bringing down the operation. This case is a prototypical example of how the Mafia 2.0 has transformed its traditional illegal operations, such as gambling, into major cybercrimes, enhancing its profits while risking monitoring by the authorities. As this and the other case studies show, cyberspace has led to new but generally ephemeral forms of organization and inter-gang cooperation (Varese, 2010). Hybrid criminality is widespread, whereby criminal planning occurs online by a small core group and carried out in real space via specific individuals or localized cells. It is a form of organized crime that is truly terrifying, given its reach and expanded criminal operations.

Epilogue

Because of cyberspace, organized crime has morphed considerably into something that could never have been anticipated by the Mafia 1.0. Nevertheless, there are still considerable continuities between the 1.0 and 2.0 versions, as discussed in this chapter. As organized criminals now plan their operations through cyberspace, they have in effect started refashioning their image to fit in with the times, using social media tools in self-serving ways, as will be discussed further in subsequent chapters. Dark markets not only make illicit goods and services available more broadly than ever before, but they also enable criminals to interact quickly and continuously with each other, making it easier to share information and resources, launder money, and largely evade detection by authorities. Organized crime groups have, in effect, merged their traditional mode of operations with online forms of criminality, becoming increasingly transnational, working together with other criminal organizations to maximize profits and enhance functionality.

However, in migrating to cyberspace, organized criminals may have exposed themselves to the scrutiny they have always shunned. An example is the case of a Mafia fugitive, Marc Feren Claude Biart, who was caught in the Caribbean after appearing on one of his YouTube cooking videos, recognized for his distinctive body tattoos. Biart was leading a secret life in Boca Chica, in the Dominican Republic, with the local Italian community considering him simply as a countryman.

Biart had been a fugitive since 2014, when Italian prosecutors ordered his arrest for trafficking in cocaine in the Netherlands on behalf of the Cacciola clan of the 'Ndrangheta. Like others of his generation, his love for cooking and his addiction to YouTube ultimately got him arrested. As Salam and Moschella (2021) have remarked, this case shows how the authorities now operate:

> Biart's arrest marks a breakthrough for the international effort led by Interpol and multiple European police forces to bring down organized crime. Known as "Interpol Cooperation Against 'Ndrangheta," the initiative launched last year is tasked with disrupting the mafia gang's global network, which Interpol says is present on every world continent.

Actually, as this case shows, some things do not change. One of these is criminal hubris. The lure of the cool and hypermasculine mobster is the same as it ever was – it is just being performed on the computer screen, as the Biart case emphasized. This has become a bone of contention between older mafiosi and the new generation of mobsters. The latter are blamed by the former of having lost respect for their historical roots and of having become too "soft," preferring their smartphones and social media platforms to their fists. According to court documents that we examined, cases such as the Biart one are increasing. One case involved an extortion plot that was foolishly announced on Twitter, along with emojis. The police were able to trace the plot to its organizational online source and thus dismantle it.

While traditional mafias' cultural tropes, codes, and rituals seem to remain untouched by time, they are actually at risk of dissipating into something heterogenous, lacking the distinct brand identity that mafiosi have always attempted to fashion for themselves. Fiction makes mafia-type organizations attractive to this day, both the fiction created by the mafiosi themselves to legitimize their lives and the fiction created by popular culture to make them look even more attractive and exceptional than they could ever have imagined. Without these dual fictions, the perception of mafias as honorable societies of heroic figures would dissipate. But on social media, the same kinds of fictions no longer apply. In this digital environment, the new generation of mafiosi seems to be more interested in showing off than in abiding by the old mythologies.

As Ivano Gabrielli, the Director of the Postal and Communications Police, a unit of Italy's state police that investigates cybercrime told us in an interview, there is little doubt that the traditional mafias are undergoing a radical transformation in the Internet Age. They have increasingly developed technological savvy to evade detection, communicating a new image of themselves to the world.

According to Gabrielli, mobsters can now be anywhere in the world, conducting operations with the click of a mouse or the touch of a screen, making it highly difficult to capture them. They are technically knowledgeable operators undergoing a "digital evolution," as he called it, setting themselves apart from the older mafiosi.

As cyber expert John Adams (2016: 6–7) has insightfully remarked, mobsters have understood that we have entered a new world in which even wars will be conducted online: "Cyber war will sooner or later replace kinetic war. Cyber war is often presented as a new kind of war that is cheaper, cleaner and less risky for an attacker than other forms of armed conflict." Mafia-type organizations have certainly taken notice of this state of affairs.

2

HYBRID CRIMINALITY

Prologue

A famous case in the early archives of hybrid organized crime goes back to late 2012. The office workers at a shipping company in the port of Antwerp in Belgium started noticing that their computers had suddenly become too slow. They also became aware that certain containers of goods were disappearing without explanation – alerting them that something was amiss. The company called in computer experts and the Belgian police, who discovered that several of their workstations had been hacked, which the police believed had taken place over two years starting in June 2011. The attack was perpetrated by a Dutch-based drug trafficking group, which hid cocaine and heroin in containers holding legitimate cargoes at the Antwerp port. The traffickers had used hackers to infiltrate the company's computer networks, giving them access to data about the location and security details of the containers. The operation took place in phases, starting with malicious software being emailed to staff members, which allowed the crime group to access the relevant information; then, with this information in hand, the traffickers would send in truck drivers to steal the cargo before the legitimate owner arrived to pick it up. After the breach was discovered initially and a firewall was installed in the shipping company computer system to prevent further attacks, the traffickers-hackers were not deterred; they broke into the premises

DOI: 10.4324/9781003278597-3

and fitted devices into the computers secretly, allowing them remote access.

The Antwerp incident has become a prototypical one showing how hybrid organized crime unfolds and what operational aspects it might entail. Criminal organizations from anywhere in the world now use hacking and other forms of intrusion into computer systems to help them plan their criminal schemes. They can then coordinate with real-world criminals to put the finishing touches on the schemes. In a phrase, hybrid criminal operations involve two groups of perpetrators: those who know how to access a computer or online data and personnel illegally and those who will then complete the task in the real world. The success of any hybrid operation depends on the level of coordination between these two groups. It is thus viable primarily for criminal organizations with sufficient finances to hire the necessary computer experts and the ground crew to carry out the physical part of the operation. Hybrid operations are thus best suited to traditional organized criminals, who have a broad experience, substantial finances, and who seek to enhance their criminal efficiency and range of activities via computer expertise. So instead of physically entering the premises and stealing the records and files of a company or an individual, cybercrime groups access them remotely by hacking computers. In addition to intrusion into specific computers, they can now extend their reach into the entire network, allowing them to remove barriers to operational success that the group might have otherwise faced. In effect, hybrid criminality has become a new virulent form of organized crime that reduces risk and increases operational efficiency.

Nonetheless, hybrid operations do not change the basic structure of mafia-type organizations. They make it more flexible and efficient, providing mobsters with a new and profitable way to plan and execute their illegal schemes. But because of this enhanced flexibility and efficiency, mafia culture is changing and adapting accordingly, often to the chagrin of the older bosses, who might lament the supposed dissolution of the traditional "values" and codes that have been intrinsic to mafia culture for centuries. Traditional organized crime might now have cyber-bosses and digital councils making crucial decisions, alongside its age-old organizational structure, with the addition of coding, malware, and social engineering departments, and money mules responsible for carrying out some of the operations in real space. It may have taken a while for traditional organized crime to adapt to this new world of the matrix, perhaps sensing that it would lose its "purity." But the new generations hold no stake in the past, reared in an era where the sense of history is tenuous at best, and are thus more inclined to adopt cutting-edge technologies to carry out their operations. As the younger mobsters have taken over the upper command ranks, the transition to hybrid criminality has occurred worldwide. This may have made the traditional mafias less organic, as criminals from different cliques band together to pool resources and expand their range of operations.

The term *hybrid*, as used in criminology, actually refers to two aspects of organized crime: (a) the coordination of online and offline operations and (b) the loosening of the previous strict criteria for membership, which was limited to ethnicity and other past real-world criteria. Actually, as Starbuck et al. (2001: 1) point out, membership hybridity goes as far back as the 1920s:

> "Hybrid" youth gangs have existed in the United States at least since the 1920s. Early hybrid gangs were described mainly as mixed-race or mixed-ethnicity gangs; modern-day hybrid gangs, however, have more diverse characteristics. "Hybrid gang culture" is characterized by members of different racial/ethnic groups participating in a single gang, individuals participating in multiple gangs, unclear rules or codes of conduct, symbolic associations with more than one well- established gang (e.g., use of colors and graffiti from different gangs), cooperation of rival gangs in criminal activity, and frequent mergers of small gangs.

As discussed in the previous chapter, this shift in organized crime structure implies adapting theories and classifications to reflect the new reality. It may no longer be practicable or meaningful to precisely pigeonhole criminal organizations according to traditional notions. As Natasha Tusikov (2012) has observed, monolithic models of organized criminal structure and value systems and codes are no longer viable, given the multifarious nature of hybrid criminality.

Hybrid Organized Crime

As organized crime researchers Leukfeldt and Holt (2019) have noted, the power of hybrid criminality, as compared to the previous geographically and ethnically constrained type, is that it is composed of loose groups of individuals who come together to perpetrate one crime, do it effectively and profitably, and then disappear, making it virtually impossible to pin them down or even to characterize their operations. While the hierarchical structure of, say, New York City's Five Families, has historical validity and can easily be described to this day, in the online world, it is virtually impossible to assign a set organizational structure to a criminal organization, given its need to adapt technologically in a continuous fashion. Different criminal organizations now enter into mutating crime-specific relationships with each other. The syndication model of the past, exemplified by the Five Families, is vastly different from the hybrid one. It meant cooperation between criminal families or groups represented by an umbrella term or brand, who would be assigned different territories of operation as a way to avoid bloody rivalries. In hybrid criminality, on the other hand, the various criminal organizations collaborate in online operations and then disassemble after a successful one. In some of the cases we examined, nonetheless, there appears to be a stable and continuous core group of criminal actors accompanied by an ancillary group who are hired for their technical expertise or for money muling tasks, on a job-to-job basis.

Hybrid criminality, which we have characterized as the Mafia 2.0, is revolutionary in terms of traditional mafias in two key ways: (a) it has diminished the reliance on a unity of operations that were essential in the real world; (b) it has loosened the emotional attachment to a symbolic identity that was once perceived as distinctive and historically determined. In today's wired world, practicality and efficiency overrule symbolism and historical value. As Manuela Bertone has also observed, traditional organized crime and other criminal organizations are currently at the center of a narrative construction that expands and feeds new stories and myths (Bertone, 2021).

So, the traditional operations of extortion, illegal gambling, drug trafficking, and the like are now more easily executed through hybrid criminal structures and methods, including online and offline operations and collaboration among disparate gangs and individuals. And even though this might subject organized crime to new risks of exposure, as evidenced by the Trojan Horse Shield case (Chapter 1), there is little doubt that cyberspace has been highly advantageous to mafia-type organizations overall. Physical tasks such as killings and land-based drug movements remain, but these are at the bottom of the list of the operational systems – carried out whenever necessary. Also, as mentioned, the online world has made it increasingly useful for the different mafias to collaborate with each other and even with terrorists. As Reggie Kramer (2021) has remarked, today the pure (historical) organized criminal groups are receding more and more, giving way to hybrid organized criminal organizations "solely for profit or survival." This situation is illustrated prototypically by the current Yakuza, which has been decimated by ever more effective laws and pressured by younger, fluid and flexible organizations, such as the Hang-Gure, literally Half-Gang, to modify its ways.

The Mafia 2.0 has embraced the newest forms of global Internet communications – a fact that some of the older mobsters see as a betrayal of their roots in the *omertà* code of the past. Crime family members now post videos on social media that often become viral – visibly breaking the code. Mafias have crossed over to the other side of the matrix, seemingly conditioned to do so by the communicative patterns and pressures of the modern world. This has created a veritable paradigm shift in virtually all areas of previous mafia operationality. For instance, the main methods of passing mafia operations and values from one generation to the next involved a top-down process, from bosses to subsequent generations. Today, the transmission is a much more complicated process since it involves new criminal actors (such as hackers) and new intergang syndications. Also, new criminal ties and activities spring up constantly, making the definition of organized crime as a unitary, singular structure increasingly obsolescent. In 2000, the UN Convention on Transnational Organized Crime defined organized crime as a group of three or more individuals who undertake serious criminal activities in some coordinated manner to obtain financial benefits, utilizing some internal organization and having existed for an extended period. While this still holds to a great extent, the definition has since been expanded to include the concept of hybridity of operations at the transnational level. A functional characterization of hybrid criminality is given by Andrea Di Nicola (2022), which is worth repeating here:

> In the digital society, very different organized crime groups coexist with different organizational models: from online cybercrime to traditional organized crime groups to hybrid criminal groups in which humans and machines "collaborate" in new and close ways in networks of human and non-human actors. These criminal groups commit very different organized crime activities, from the most technological to the most traditional,

and move from online to offline. They use technology and interact with computers for a variety of purposes, and the distinction between the physical and virtual dimensions of organized crime is increasingly blurred.

Mafia-type organizations have traditionally ensured their perpetuity by embedding themselves into their native society as parallel cultures (with their own founding myths, symbols, codes of honor and secrecy, codes of inter-clan communication, and so on), forging corrupt alliances with politicians, lawyers, judges, businessmen, and police officers, and demanding strict conformity in behavior from clan members. But the Mafia 2.0 does not depend exclusively on operations carried out on a native soil, as discussed. This has not, however, attenuated the ability of organized crime groups such as the Calabrian 'Ndrangheta to continue exploiting victims directly within their socio-geographical worlds. At the same time, however, they have established branches abroad, maintaining communications through unreachable sectors of the Dark Web, and allowing computer experts into the fold often recruited apart from its blood-based criteria for membership. The advantages of hybridity became obvious to all the traditional criminal organizations in the twenty-first century's first decade, highlighted by the case of the anonymous 2008 Mariposa site, which offered for sale a malware program that allowed its users to monitor activities for passwords, information on bank credentials, and credit cards wherever it was installed. The malware would then attempt to self-propagate itself to other connectible arrangement using various botnet systems, such as contacting a command-and-control server within the botnet. Although no identifiable organized crime group was ever identified as running the site, it certainly caught the attention of traditional organized crime. It showed, overall, that the mafias could enter the world of the matrix to expand their previous extortion schemes immensely, opening up opportunities that would have been inconceivable, or at least impractical, in the past, from identity theft to transmitting contraband across borders through Internet communications.

Another key aspect differentiating traditional mafias from the hybrid ones today is that the members show no qualms of conscience whatsoever in presenting themselves to the world via the Internet, a form of exposure that would have been taboo in the past, given the codes of secrecy that all mafias saw as intrinsic to their operations. As a specific case in point, consider the Facebook page, "Honour and

Dignity," maintained by 'Ndrangheta boss Vincenzo Torcasio, before he was sent to prison in 2017. In addition to trivial everyday messages and quotations from Oscar Wilde, Paulo Coelho, and Albert Einstein, Torcasio posted pictures of large sums of money accompanied by the words: "when this is involved, you can't trust anyone." In a short time, Torcasio became a social media influencer, gaining notoriety on the Internet. As the police officers we have contacted emphasized, cases such as this are now common, allowing the authorities to use social media platforms to monitor, track, and mine the criminals for evidentiary materials. As one police investigator quipped, it would seem that the criminals have traded their fists for hashtags and their *pizzini* (small slips of paper that the Sicilian Mafia used for high-level communications) for social media captions. As the Torcasio case shows, the new bosses are increasingly embracing technology to shape their criminal brands, adapting them to the communicative and lifestyle patterns of the Internet Age. Of course, in the pre-Internet Age, crime bosses also loved the limelight. Al Capone introduced the Hollywood look of a well-dressed gangster who would revel in showing himself off to the cameras. Former New York City mobster John Gotti was even called "Dapper Don" because he too sought publicity and media attention in the 1980s with his expensive designer clothes and slick appearance. But because of the fact that both had become public celebrities, they attracted unwanted attention from the police – a situation that would eventually help to bring them down. Fast forwarding to today, similar criminal public figures would be considered anachronistic ludicrous caricatures. The move to social media to show off, on the other hand, is in line with the broad spread of narcissism in the current age.

Hybrid criminality has produced a "dualistic" gangster (Chapter 1) who operates secretly on the Dark Web but presents himself brazenly to the global public on social media. The mafioso today has one foot in the Dark Web and the other on the luminous surface Internet. This raises several questions: If hybrid-based criminality has allowed organized criminals to become physically detached from customers and victims, will the members become more disconnected from each other as well? Is the dualistic character of the young mafioso signaling the demise of the traditional mafias in terms of their age-old criminal structure, identity-conserving strategies, and overall lifestyle patterns? Is the ephemerality of the operations and the technologies used affecting the ability of mafias to sustain themselves in their social milieu? To the point of the foregoing discussion, Europol (2018) reported that almost one-third of known criminal networks exist for only a short period of time and are set up to support specific illegal schemes, after which they either retreat into previous forms of organization or dissipate completely.

As the United Nations Office on Drugs and Crime (UNODC) (2018) has also noted, contemporary organized criminal groups are more fluid in their composition and structure than they ever were, reflecting "a wider characteristic in society in general, where long-term personal relationships diminish, reducing personal loyalty and commitment among individuals and institutions." Ironically, as UNODC goes on to observe, "illicit acts committed by organized criminal groups have remained quite stable, reflecting changes in the opportunities to provide illicit goods and services." UNODC identified four types of criminal organizations, offline and online, which can be illustrated as shown in Figure 2.1.

The *hierarchical* model is the traditional one, with the bosses at the top to whom allegiance must be pledged unconditionally, under threat of death. Members of the clans are seen as "family." Each clan within the Sicilian Mafia, the Calabrian 'Ndrangheta, the Japanese Yakuza, and the Chinese Triads, among others, has operated as hierarchical organization. The *local cultural model* is adaptive to situations and new contextual conditions. So while ethnicity is still a requirement for membership, the groups are more flexible in the criteria of selection and organization. Such organizations include the Neapolitan

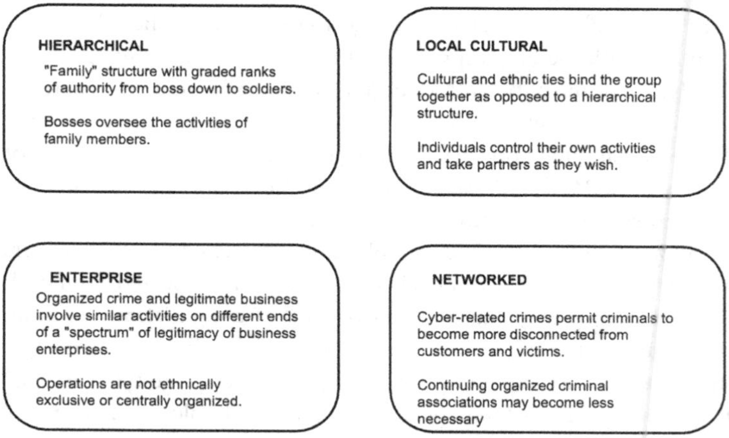

HIERARCHICAL

"Family" structure with graded ranks of authority from boss down to soldiers.

Bosses oversee the activities of family members.

LOCAL CULTURAL

Cultural and ethnic ties bind the group together as opposed to a hierarchical structure.

Individuals control their own activities and take partners as they wish.

ENTERPRISE

Organized crime and legitimate business involve similar activities on different ends of a "spectrum" of legitimacy of business enterprises.

Operations are not ethnically exclusive or centrally organized.

NETWORKED

Cyber-related crimes permit criminals to become more disconnected from customers and victims.

Continuing organized criminal associations may become less necessary

FIGURE 2.1 Models of Organized Crime

Camorra. *Enterprise* or business model emerges from taking advantage of opportunities that present themselves at specific points in time; outlaw motorcycle gangs and various drug cartels fall into this category. *Networked* structures are the hybrid ones that coordinate their activities and adapt their organizational structure to an online–offline dynamic. The main features associated with these organized crime groups include the following (based on Europol's 2016 report):

*   *Crime-as-a-Service*: these hire people who know how to use computer, cybercrime tools, and services as needed.
*   *Ransomware*: these use ransomware and Trojans (malicious programs used to obtain confidential information about customers and clients using online banking and payment systems) as their major extortion schemes.
*   *Criminal Use of Data*: the collection of data is a key commodity for the hybrid criminals, procured through various digital techniques (such as phishing and hacking), allowing them to carry out lucrative fraud and extortion schemes.
*   *Payment Fraud*: a common operation involves credit card and ATM fraud, which is easily carried out and thus used for financing other types of hybrid criminality.
*   *Online Sexual Abuse:* the use of end-to-end encrypted platforms for sharing media, coupled with the help of largely anonymous payment systems, has led to an escalation in the live streaming of sexual abuse events.
*   *The Dark Web*: the Dark Web has enabled criminals to become involved in a wide range of illicit activities, as the Mariposa case brought out (Chapter 1); overall, the availability of cybercrime tools and services allows hybrid criminality to spread and thrive.
*   *Social Engineering*: expertise in extortion methods based on phishing has spiraled since the emergence of hybrid criminality already in the first decade of the twenty-first century; social engineering is the manipulation of people into performing actions or divulging confidential information.
*   *Virtual Currencies*: cryptocurrencies such as bitcoin are the currency systems that fuel the digital underground economy.

Other kinds of online criminal activities have emerged in the era of the Dark Web, some of which will be elaborated subsequently. Suffice it to say that the new activities have greatly bolstered the coffers of criminals – hence their desire to enter the online underground economy. Moreover, the growing misuse of legitimate encryption services for illegal purposes, as one police officer we interviewed emphasized, has become a serious impediment to the detection, investigation, and prosecution of hybrid criminals.

Cyber Gangs

As Weber and Kruisbergen (2019: 3) remark, there is little doubt that the world of organized crime has changed in the Millennium, as criminal markets on the Dark Web have increasingly become the mainstay of the major criminal organizations:

> An important part of organized crime activities boils down to the sale and distribution of illegal goods and services. Recent years have shown important, technology-driven changes on criminal markets. Developments in information technology, namely the use of cryptocurrencies such as Bitcoin, encryption software, and secured browser technology such as TOR (The Onion Router), facilitated the widespread use of so-called dark web markets, such as AlphaBay or Silk Road. Marketplaces such as these allow demand and supply of illegal goods to meet online, which of course constituted a major innovation of criminal markets.

The online world has been genuinely opportunistic for criminal organizations, allowing them to expand their activities considerably. One of these is phishing, the fraudulent practice of sending emails purporting to be from reputable companies or individuals to get people to reveal personal information, such as passwords and credit card numbers. Another is the threat of publicly revealing embarrassing or incriminating personal information about someone if money is not paid to the scammer. And the third is hacking an individual or an organization to gather private information and potential vulnerabilities, which criminal organizations then use to contact the victim with evidence of the breach to demand ransom. Identity theft has also become a primary illegal operation, involving malicious software to obtain the desired information directly from the user's computer. This then allows for intercepting communications, identifying log-in keyboard strokes, and recording entries made by a user. Apart from direct financial profit, criminals can use the identity-related information for other purposes, such as using a victim's bank account to launder money. Cyberspace has also led to a revision of the traditional recruits to criminal organizations. Crime bosses have come to understand that to conduct crime operations today, they will require computer-trained experts in addition to their usual muscle-bound enforcers.

The global effects of transnational organized cybercrime cannot be underestimated. It now undermines governments and social stability in some countries, having become wide-ranging, paying no regard to national boundaries. The victim of a sex trafficking scheme may come from one country, be transported through another, and finally sold in a third country. Cyberspace has even produced its own new types of criminal gangs, which have no connection to traditional organized crime. The following are some examples:

- The *Cobalt Cybercrime Gang*, based in Russia, attacks financial firms across the globe; it is the online equivalent of the traditional bank heist gangs, stealing money without the need for guns. The suspected ringleader was apprehended in 2018, but authorities believe the gang is still intact after witnessing similar attacks on several institutions after his capture.
- The *Lazarus Group*, with ties to North Korea, carries out cyberattacks on organizations and institutions. The most well-known ones were the Sony Pictures hack in 2014 and the WannaCry cyberattack in 2017, which crippled England's National Health Service.
- The *MageCart Syndicate* comprises various gangs from different areas, whose primary activity is stealing consumer and credit card information by intercepting payment services on e-commerce websites. Several well-known examples of the group's activities were its breach of British Airways' data in 2018, compromising the financial and personal information of over 380,000 people, its skimming operation against hardware vendor Newegg also in 2018, and its breach of Ticketmaster data in the same year, which exposed the personal information of over 40,000 customers.
- The *Evil Corp*, located in Russia, utilizes computer viruses to attack American and European institutions, with Dridex malware, which hides its coding within seemingly harmless data. The gang has even posted videos on social media of its leaders parading their extravagant lifestyles, gaining temporary fame throughout cyberspace.

- The dismantled *GozNym Gang*, which used a powerful Trojan malware, was a worldwide cybercrime network. Its name is a portmanteau of *Nymaim* and *Gozi* malware, which can infiltrate a victim's email attachments or URLs undetected, lying in wait for the victim to log into a bank account. The funds are then laundered via money mules, who transfer them in person, through a courier service, or electronically on behalf of the gang.
- The *DarkSide*, which has become notorious for halting the U.S. Colonial Pipeline's fuel distribution system in 2021, causing gasoline supply shortages, primarily targets large corporations, which are more inclined to shell out ransom money if their services are disrupted. DarkSide is a "cyber-gun for hire," so to speak, executing ransomware assaults for hire, with the illegal proceeds split between the perpetrator and the software mastermind. It is another example of a "crime-as-a-service" provider.
- *REvil*, based in Russia, became infamous for hacking Quanta Computer, a Taiwanese business that assembles Apple computers. REvil illegally obtained technical data about upcoming Apple devices and used it to demand ransom money from the company. After an attack, REvil would threaten to publish the information on their "Happy Blog" page unless the ransom was received. It was dismantled in 2022.
- The *Clop* was a ransomware site, launched in 2019, managed by a gang specializing in "double-extortion" – paying a ransom in return for a decryption key that would allow the victimized company to regain access to stolen information, but would have to pay an additional ransom to prevent the data from being made public.
- The *FIN7*, another Russian-based organization, which has been operational since 2012, is one of the most successful organized cybercrime syndicates in cyberspace. Its security breaches have involved "cross-attack" schemes, whereby a cyberattack is used for several objectives, such as facilitating ransomware extortion while enabling the perpetrator to exploit the stolen data by selling it to another party. In 2017, it was accused of being behind a cyberattack on corporations in the Securities and Exchange Commission in the United States. The data was utilized to extort a ransom, which was subsequently invested in the legitimate stock market.

The world of online organized crime has branched out in many new directions, allowing for new gangs to emerge, with no connections to any founding mythology, code of conduct, initiation rites, and so on – all of which have always differentiated traditional organized crime from street thugs or random criminals. Anyone can become a member of an online gang – all that is needed is computer expertise. As a result, cyberspace is now inhabited by traditional criminal organizations, which have developed digital expertise on their own; new gangs, who have taken their expertise and applied it fruitfully to perpetrate cybercrimes; and a host of other criminal actors who can hide on the other side of the screen, receding into its darker regions. As Lunde (2004: 49) perceptively noted, the reason hybrid cyber-criminality has spread so broadly is easy to understand: "While many people work from home, using a computer, it is just as easy and convenient for criminals to do likewise." Traditional Mafias have quickly learned that they can now engage in their usual activities – fraud, extortion, money laundering, drug trafficking, planning revenges – from an easy chair at their homes in front of a computer screen.

In summary, the world of the matrix has expanded the range and constitution of organized crime, radically affecting its age-old practices. The Mafia 2.0 has little regard for history and traditions – it is interested in making money and gaining power through the new opportunities offered by cyberspace. Cyberspace has also made crime itself a form of spectacle. As Lessley Anderson (2012) has argued, today, viewing crime live on a social media platform such as YouTube has become a sort of fetishized obsession, allowing criminals to become dark celebrities of sorts, attractive to potential recruits.

In this digital environment, anyone can become a criminal. A well-known example is AlphaBay, a trafficking Dark Web marketplace launched in 2014 by Canadian Alexandre Cazes, who used the pseudonym of Rawmeo. This case shows how one single person can, by himself, set up a criminal network online with ease. AlphaBay was, in fact, one of the largest portals in the history of cybercrime, selling more illegal drugs, guns, stolen credit cards, controlled substances, fraudulent identification documents, counterfeit goods, malware, fire-arms, and toxic chemicals than the Silk Road site it mimicked. In May 2015, the site announced access to integrated digital contracts and escrow systems. AlphaBay was also noteworthy for accepting other cryptocurrencies in addition to bitcoin. It is mindboggling to reflect on how anyone acting alone can scam countless victims by just sitting in front of a screen. More than 200,000 buyers worldwide had accessed the AlphaBay site before being brought down in 2017 by a consortium of international police agencies (Anselmi, 2019).

Cryptocurrency

Cryptocurrency is the financial lifeblood of cybercriminality. Without it, cybercrimes would be impracticable to carry out successfully. Cryptocurrencies are the nexus between online and offline operations, allowing for the onion routing of funds over computer networks. In an onion network, messages are composed with layers of encryption, analogous to layers of an onion – hence the metaphor. The data is transmitted through network nodes called onion routers, each of which "peels" away a particular layer, uncovering the data's next destination. At its final destination, the message's final layer is decrypted. The sender remains anonymous throughout because each intermediary knows only the location of the immediately preceding and following layers. As Europol (2022: 5) has put it, cryptocurrency makes such networks functional:

> In 2009, Bitcoin emerged as the first traditional virtual currency. While existing virtual currencies had traditional entities as intermediaries, this new currency became popular because of the absence of third parties in the transactions. Its use of online technologies combined with cryptography resulted in a completely new transfer system where a secure payment could be sent directly without the use of an intermediary, such as a central bank or public authority. Due to its dependence on cryptography, this type of currency is commonly referred to as cryptocurrency.

Bitcoin is "digital cash," allowing for anonymous payments, free of brokerage fees. Its creator, known by the pseudonym of Satoshi Nakamoto, wanted to make available a new currency capable of transferring purchasing power independently of financial intermediaries. As Pieroni (2018) has perceptively remarked: "The rise of cryptocurrency has given organized crime a new look, swapping society's Kuklinskis and Capones for pseudonymous sleuths and computer-clad criminals, and underground operations for 'dark web' schemes that transcend international borders at the click of a button." As Nolasco Braaten and

Vaughan (2021) have aptly commented, cryptocurrency has provided new opportunistic ways for anyone to engage in online criminality outside of direct physical (and risky) involvement (Gottschalk, 2019).

As our law enforcement sources discussed with us, the unlawful use of cryptocurrencies nevertheless entails many risks, which they have themselves witnessed. The reason is that, unlike fiat currencies, cryptocurrencies are subject to high volatility. Fiat currencies are those that are not backed by any commodity such as gold or silver, but simply decreed by governments to be legal tender; that is, they do not have intrinsic value – only to individuals who use them as a medium of exchange, agreeing on their real monetary value. Criminal networks are reluctant to entrust their illegally gained funds to unpredictable currencies in contrast to the stability of conventional cash flows. But they are aware of the many advantages that such currencies offer in the overall scheme of their operations, such as money laundering – the main criminal activity associated with the illicit use of cryptocurrencies. The following are the steps cybercriminals employ for laundering funds on a blockchain – a system in which a record of transactions made in a cryptocurrency is maintained across several computers linked in a peer-to-peer network. To conceal the illegitimate origin of payments, criminals use a variety of strategies in the money laundering process.

- *Placement*: This is the phase when illicit crypto funds are brought into an organized criminal group's financial system through intermediaries such as online gambling sites. Funds can be bought with specific online cryptocurrency exchanges or with real cash.
- *Layering*: This is the phase when criminals obscure the source of their funds through structured transactions, making the trail of illegal funds difficult to trace, converting one type of cryptocurrency into another, as long as it is needed to do so. Criminals can also move their cryptocurrency holdings to another country.
- *Integration*: During this phase, the illegal money is inserted into the regular economy, where it can gain a clean status. One of the most common techniques is the use of over-the-counter brokers as intermediaries between buyers and sellers of cryptocurrencies.

What makes online money laundering particularly effective, vis-à-vis the offline money laundering tactics of the past, is the anonymous and untraceable services and networks that the online venue affords.

One of these is the "crypto mixing" service, also known as a tumbler, which allows users to conduct transactions by mixing their crypto-currencies with other users. A typical transaction takes cryptocurrencies from a client, sends them through a series of addresses, and then recombines them into "clean cryptos." Criminals can also use peer-to-peer networks, which are decentralized networks for transmitting funds to a different location, such as another country with lax anti-money laundering legislation. These exchanges, called nested services, are part of a blockchain that allows for converting crypto-currency into fiat or even real currency. On the blockchain ledger, the nested transactions appear as having been conducted by their host counterparties rather than by the hosted nested services. Gambling platforms are commonly used for cryptocurrency money laundering. Funds are paid into a platform through anonymous accounts, either cashed out or placed in bets. Once the money in the account is paid out, it can be given legal status.

Cryptocurrencies are also the payment of choice for criminal commodities and services, such as drugs purchased online, such as in Dark Web marketplaces, where they are the exclusive means of payment. Also, extortion schemes carried out by cybercriminals now make extensive use of cryptocurrencies. As Europol (2022: 7) has noted, however, it is in the area of money laundering that cryptocurrencies have given the greatest advantage to organized crime, since the networks in a blockchain can rely on established infrastructure such as bank accounts. As such, they have become the new source for enhancing the power and reach of the Mafia 2.0:

> Money laundering networks provide their services to other criminal networks, which may include the acquisition or trade of cryptocurrencies, the traditional type of criminal assets and the final cash out in the accounts of criminals. Professional money laundering networks are a significant threat and enable other criminal networks to operate. Marketplaces on the dark web advertise money laundering cryptocurrency service providers. They also offer information on how criminals can cash out cryptocurrencies, such as by exchanging Bitcoin for gift vouchers or prepaid debit cards.

As our police sources relayed to us, confirming the Europol report, tackling online money laundering is tantamount to fighting organized crime at its core. Paying constant attention to transactions to and from countries with higher incidences of organized crime is also a key anti-crime strategy. The investigators are no longer just detectives; they are now increasingly becoming experts in global trends in financial systems, as cases involving cryptocurrencies have shown – for instance, U.S. v. Colldock 2017; U.S. v. Michell 2018; and U.S. v. Reuer 2019 (Nolasco Braaten and Vaughan, 2021).

As Europol has amply documented (Europol, 2022), online criminality, based on cryptocurrencies, has made previous offline schemes, such as the infamous Ponzi one, more expansive. An example is the takedown by Europol, Swiss Federal Police, and Belgian Federal Judicial Police of an online organized crime group running a worldwide Ponzi scheme using the social media platform "Vitae.co" and the website "Vitaetoken.io" in 2021. Over 200,000 individuals from 177 countries have fallen victim to the investment scam. The crime group members were mainly Belgian nationals using a company under Swiss jurisdiction. As our police sources told us, this case is hardly exceptional. For example, the Camorra in Naples will supply drugs to street-level dealers to sell them for cash. A courier then collects the money from the dealers and delivers it to a broker who arranges for it to be converted into bitcoin and then sent to an address specified by the crime group, for a fee. Similar schemes are utilized by other Italian mafias and, indeed, by other mafias throughout the world.

As Europol (2022) discovered from its research on the financial activities of cyber organized gangs:

- Cryptocurrencies are the payment method of choice for criminals; however, since they are highly volatile, there is a reluctance by some cyber gangs and traditional mafias to use them for long-term investments.
- Illicit funds travel through a multistep process involving financial entities, many of which are not part of the standard, regulated financial markets.
- Since transactions are logged onto the blockchain, they are publicly available, making them traceable. As a result, law enforcement can access illegal money exchanges involving cryptocurrency more easily than it can with cash transactions.
- By turning money raised illegally into cryptocurrency and then using it in illegal parts of the Internet, mafias can launder money without attracting notice (most of the time).

Interestingly, in some cases, there is even a return to a barter system, involving the exchange of weapons for minerals such as coltan, which is essential for the manufacture of technological devices, such as mobile phones and computers. The 'Ndrangheta was one of the first criminal organizations to buy coltan by paying for it with weapons in the Democratic Republic of Congo. Equally sought after is cobalt, from which tantalum is obtained, and used for missile systems and mobile telephony.

McLuhan's Four Laws

To summarize, the aim of the foregoing discussion has been to portray the Mafia 2.0 as an opportunistic hybrid criminal syndicate, which has emerged because of the practicality and reach of operations that cyberspace permits, even if this has entailed a diminishment of the historical brand image and an attenuation in the value or sustainability of previous codes of honor and secrecy. The emergence of hybrid organized crime signals a veritable paradigm shift that has no parallels in the archives of organized crime. While the past is still retrieved in the present constitution of criminal organizations, it is rendered less relevant than it ever was. In effect, organized crime has been subjected to McLuhan's four laws of media (see McLuhan and McLuhan, 1988), which are worth revisiting here in the framework of hybrid criminality. The laws – amplification, obsolescence, reversal, and retrieval – seem to describe the effects of the migration to cyberspace on the part of the traditional organized groups rather insightfully.

McLuhan claimed that a new technology or invention will at first amplify some sensory, intellectual, or other human faculty. While one area is amplified, another is lessened or rendered obsolescent until it is used to maximum capacity, whence it reverses its characteristics and is retrieved in another way. Consider the case of the 'Ndrangheta, one of the mafias that clings stubbornly to traditions while understanding the practicality and power of cyberspace operations, which have amplified its operationality considerably. Today, this criminal organization can coordinate its criminal schemes in an online–offline pattern and can enter into temporary partnerships with other criminal groups, to great advantage, no matter where or who they are. This has rendered previous traditional ways of running their operations on the ground, from extortion to racketeering obsolescent, albeit not completely eradicated, since they continue to be retrieved, whenever the situation calls for it, or else even reversed, as when the online venue is abandoned to avoid monitoring. The case of the 'Ndrangheta is a capsule of how McLuhan's laws apply to hybrid mafia-type organizations. A new system, such as cryptocurrency, does indeed amplify the ways in which money laundering and other criminal activities are now carried out, rendering offline financial schemes obsolescent. However, a retrieval of previous money-laundering practices remains an option if a situation demands it.

An interesting case in point of retrieval within an organized crime operation is the 2018 one involving a takedown operation of the 'Ndrangheta in the Netherlands, Italy, Germany, Belgium, and Luxembourg (Eurojust, 2018). The operation, which was code-named "Pollino," led to the seizure of thousands of kilos of drugs worth over two million euros. The relevant aspect of this case was that the authorities had intercepted a conversation in which a broker linked to the 'Ndrangheta stated that he was willing to pay with bitcoin. But the Brazilian narcos involved in the same operation refused the offer bluntly, preferring the older method of cash. This might ordinarily seem ironically old-fashioned, but the concept of retrieval suggests that clinging on past modes of operation is based on distrust of the new ways.

The notion of the *tetrad* was introduced by McLuhan's late son, Eric (McLuhan and McLuhan, 1988), as a model to represent the operation of the four laws – that is, it is meant to show concretely how the four laws operate simultaneously. For example, applying the tetrad to a traditional organized crime syndicate will show how cyberspace amplifies, obsolesces, retrieves, and reverses various features, traits, and interactions associated with organized crime.

The different quadrants are organically intertwined (Figure 2.2) – so, once an amplification occurs, such as the enhanced range of criminality that cyberspace affords, previous land-based activities become obsolescent but are soon retrieved in various ways. A mafia group such as the 'Ndrangheta has become an international organization, adept at rechanneling the spoils gained from criminal activities into legitimate venues because of the amplifications of their actions made possible by the online medium. At the same time, it holds on to its traditions, fearing that it would become an identity-less entity. Other mafias, such as the Triads or the Vory v Zakone, have also evolved according to the tetrad. As they have amplified their criminal activities, they have also shown a tendency to retrieve elements of their historical

AMPLIFIES	OBSOLESCES
• Networking among criminals in cyberspace. • Decentralization of information sources, allowing the criminal organization more anonymity. • Speed and range of criminal activities. • Access to the global village and its institutions, from banks to casinos. • Access to connected intelligence systems and powerful software materials that can be applied to conduct criminal affairs effectively and efficiently. • Virtual communities which, together with real-world communities, expand the reach of the criminal organization for purposes of criminality.	• Previous restrictions of time and space that characterized the conduct of criminal activities in geographical space. • National boundaries are obliterated, so that a specific criminal organization can now reach anyone, anywhere on the globe. • The need for physical operations, including face-to-face intimidation, since many of these can be carried out virtually. • The need to rigidly apply historically-based processes to new members, who are now Internet-savvy and may no longer aspire to be part of a historical paradigm, but rather to bring the mafias forward in time to conform to the new realities of life in the word of the matrix.
REVERSES INTO	RETRIEVES
• Obsession with the past, as can be seen how traditional crime groups such as the 'Ndrangheta cling on to their traditions and ethnic filters for membership, despite the migration to cyberspace. • Reliance on codes of past, albeit in increasingly attenuated and nostalgic ways. • A new emphasis of values associated with traditional codes of conduct, such as *omertà*.	• Traditional identity symbols and languages (such as the Calabrian dialect in the case of the 'Ndrangheta). • A new sense of tribalism, which has not been diluted by cyberspace, as the often ostentatious online videos posted by the mafiosi on sites such as Facebook, Instagram, TikTok, or YouTube show. • Local activism in recruiting new members, complementing the efforts online.

FIGURE 2.2 Criminological Tetrad

image – a fact that is reinforced by popular culture. The number of films and videogames based on the traditional images related to Triads, and Yakuza, for example, is quite large. Most revolve around a display of martial arts skills and the pseudo-legends surrounding how they came into being. In the videogame Sleeping Dogs, set in Hong Kong, a player can assume the role of an undercover police officer on a mission to infiltrate the Triads, with his virtual pugilistic skills, matching the martial art skills of the virtual Triads' members. Retrieval in such cases is fictional.

The tetrad provides a framework for explaining why and how traditional organized crime has adapted to modern technology. It leaves behind practices and ideas that no longer fit in a while, occasionally retrieving some of them. The tetrad also provides a basis for understanding why transnational organized crime has become a frightening reality, amplifying its international reach. The central hub of power is now more likely to be a system of networks and cells, rather than clans and identifiable groups, which are better suited to carrying out hybrid operations, whereby the online components of a network allow the criminals to target victims from anywhere in the world. Then, the land-based foot soldiers carry out the necessary activities case-by-case basis. Technology has also amplified the range of criminal activities of traditional organized crime – activities that would have been unthinkable in any previous era, including art and theft and healthcare fraud, which are organized and even executed through the online medium. As the tetrad implies, the traditional mafias have attempted to retain their traditional identities and membership criteria as much as possible. Still, even in this area, they have had to adapt considerably given the need to hire individuals with expertise in technology who may have no historical–ethnic ties to the clan and to form alliances with various other global crime networks. In "The Rise of the Cyber-Mercenaries," Neri Zilber (2018) offers the following assessment of hybrid criminality and its connection to computer technology:

> Everything is becoming a computer – your phone, your fridge, your microwave, your car. The internet, which came of age in the 1970s and 1980s, was never designed with security in mind. So everyone is now scrambling to play catch-up, patching holes in both information systems (e.g., software programs) and operating systems (e.g., physical industrial plants) that are outdated, poorly written, or simply insecure.

In McLuhan's (1967) book, *The Medium is the Massage: An Inventory of Effects*, co-authored with Quentin Fiore, the spelling "massage" in the title was purported to have been a printing error rather than an intentional decision; but McLuhan liked it and it was kept as such, reflecting his initial idea of using this term to convey that any new medium has the same effect on the mind that a massage has on the body. He elaborates this view as follows (McLuhan and Fiore, 1967: 26):

> All media work us over completely. They are so persuasive in their personal, political, economic, aesthetic, psychological, moral, ethical, and social consequences that they leave no part of us untouched, unaffected, unaltered. The medium is the massage. Any understanding of social and cultural change is impossible without a knowledge of the way media work as environments. All media are extensions of some human faculty – psychic or physical.

The core lesson to be learned from McLuhan's laws of media about criminological theory is that technology affects the course of organized crime – to paraphrase McLuhan, it has worked it over completely. It is inconceivable today to think of any criminal organization existing exclusively in its traditional forms, carrying out only geographically based illegal activities. Mafia-type organizations, like everyone else living today, have had to adapt to the world of matrix. Cases like the 2015 one in which a Sicilian-based crime ring with links to Cosa Nostra was working with hackers in other countries to steal credit card information have become the norm. Brought down by an operation dubbed "Free Money," the 24 people arrested used cloned credit card codes and money laundering, setting up fictitious car rental companies and using hacked credit card information to run them in the name of the victims, who were mainly United States citizens. The group, based in Palermo, worked with hackers in Russia and Romania to harvest the card details for the scam. For the Mafiosi, this was a previously unused channel of extortion and funding. As our police sources relayed, even die-hard traditional Italian mafia groups have increasingly engaged in projects such as this one, which relies on one criminal organization working with other such organizations and with foreign criminal organizations more broadly – thus literally amplifying their base of operations.

While McLuhan himself never applied his ideas to crime, nor has the tetrad been applied by criminologists to understand the rise of hybrid criminality, as far as we know, our point here is that it fills a gap in current theoretical paradigms about criminality in the Internet Age. A tetradic analysis enables us to examine more concretely how new technologies shape organized crime and to understand how and why criminal operations become amplified while previous practices are retained to preserve those core tenets that have guided them in the past.

Case Studies: II

The cases discussed here are intended to exemplify how hybrid criminality unfolds, and how elements of cybercriminality have surfaced in concrete ways, highlighting the connection between organized crime and computer-based technologies. Cases like these are sprouting up everywhere, posing challenges to authorities that are now engaging in new kinds of training and developing technical skills. Cases such as these illustrate how computer skills have become critical to mobsters and investigators alike. As Marker (2017) – a member of the FBI – has similarly stressed:

> All of those significant criminal activities have in common the fact that they become easier to accomplish and more efficient when technology is leveraged to facilitate them . . . criminals are utilizing high tech tools developed by others and taking advantage of particularly sophisticated functionality available via the Internet. These tools and technologies are determining the future of organized crime investigations.

Case Study: The Mariposa Botnet

As mentioned previously, the Mariposa botnet case is an early example of how powerful digital tools can be made readily available to organized crime groups. The botnet was discovered in December 2008 and dismantled in 2009. It was originally created with a malware program called "Butterfly Bot," which was itself made available for purchase by criminals themselves. It contained around 12 million unique IP addresses, making it one of the largest botnets ever. After it was installed on a computer, the malware enabled the monitoring of passwords for bank accounts and credit cards, after which it would self-propagate to connected systems, contacting a main server within the botnet, monitored by its controllers, allowing it to issue orders to the botnet itself. It permitted denial-of-service attacks, email spamming, identity theft, and other cyberscamming tactics. As Sully and Thompson (2010: 18) remarked:

> The most dangerous capability of this botnet is that arbitrary executable programs are downloaded and executed on command. This allows the bot master to infinitely extend the functionality of the malicious software beyond what is implemented during the initial compromise. In addition, the malware can be updated on command to a new variant of the binary, effectively reducing or eliminating the detection rates of traditional host detection methods.

The case showed the extent to which new technology has made high-value victims easy targets, enlarging the reach of criminal actors, since the botnet attacks were able to spread exponentially through the automation capacities of the malware. Criminal organizations instantly realized how profitable and easy cyberscamming operations were, superseding the old forms of extortion and fraud. In the past, those who were extorted preferred not to make a fuss, agreeing to pay the *pizzo* (protection money) as part of the expense of running a business, given that refusing to pay would entail having the business vandalized, burned down, or else the owner being subjected to physical torture and even death. The Mariposa case showed how easy it is to extract money from victims without resorting to real-world violence. Botnets quickly entered the organized criminals' lexicon and operational toolbox shortly after the Mariposa site was shut down. The case came again before the U.S. Department of Justice in 2019, given that the authorities had discovered that the founder of the site, Matzaz Skorjanc, conspired to market a new version of Mariposa called Nice-Hash, likely on Darkode, a cybercrime forum, after being released from his five-year prison stay for the original operation. NiceHash allowed consumers to sell their computing power to assist others in mining virtual currencies. When millions in bitcoin vanished, the justice department stepped in to investigate.

Botnets are one of the most significant criminal digital systems, especially since they are being constantly improved by hackers, becoming more and more immune to detection and debugging. Mariposa showed how botnet architecture could make an individual a powerful criminal without any need to join an existing organized crime group or use physical violence.

Case Study: The GozNym Cybercrime Group

The GozNym group – a self-styled online syndicate headquartered in Russia and Georgia – was one of the most terrifying cyberspace gangs in the annals of cybercrime, whose activities were first detected in 2016 (Arghire, 2019). The group developed malware to infect victims' computers, stealing bank login passwords, which were then used to access bank accounts. Dismantling the group involved the coordinated effort of police agencies from the United States, Georgia, Ukraine, Moldova, Germany, and Bulgaria. Ten individuals were eventually brought to justice. It is estimated that over 41,000 victims, primarily businesses and financial institutions, lost money to the GozNym network.

The case showcased how a neophyte criminal organization, which originated directly online, can operate efficiently and profitably without any ties to previously existing criminal groups, becoming a general model for other gangs to emulate. The GozNym's complex operations involved several layers of criminal actors with specific duties.

The first layer consisted of two people, the network's leader and a malware developer. The developer created and managed the banking malware. Once installed on a computer, it became a keylogger, hijacking the victims' web browsers and sites by injecting phishing fields into them when they attempted to log in. The malware also included a field in the browser designed to dupe victims into using their private information in real time. The group's leader was responsible for overseeing its operations and controlling the thousands of infected computers in the botnet. The accomplices in the network were individuals recruited to provide specialized services and skills, such as coding. Then there were the "crypters," who possessed the technical expertise that allowed the gang to "cover its tracks," improving the malware's ability to evade detection. The "spammers" were responsible for creating email phishing campaigns. With the appropriate information (such as passwords), the money was then withdrawn from banks and ATMs by money mules.

The structure of the GozNym network became a model for all kinds of hybrid cybercriminal organizations. Law enforcement's description of the GozNym group as a "unified crew" was an interesting one, since most defendants were actually freelancers who offered their services via cybercrime forums. However, they coalesced into a cohesive group gradually as the criminal activities became highly lucrative, increasing the desire to stay united. A spokesperson for the FBI stated, upon making the arrests (reported in Greenberg, 2019): "The GozNym network was formed when these individuals were recruited from these online forums and came together to use their specialized skills in furtherance of the conspiracy," and as a result, "the group appears to have coordinated their activities over online chat."

Case Study: Operation Fontana-Almabahía

As our police sources confirmed to us (Chapter 1), having been involved directly in the case called Operation Fontana-Almabahía from the investigative angle, the takedown of a hybrid clan called Casamonica showed how criminal organizations have evolved into an audacious consortium of cyber-operators. The Casamonicas had been operating in the region of Castelli Romani around the Latium coast of Italy, involved in racketeering, extortion, trafficking, kidnapping, homicides, and usury for decades, until they started cooperating with other groups in online criminal activities. Law enforcement in Italy was joined by the police in Spain to take them down, along with their criminal partners, after discovering that the consortium was laundering millions of euros via hacking operations and violent coercion across Italy, Spain, Germany, Lithuania, Ireland, and the U.K. The consortium was a hybrid one, consisting of the Casamonica clan, the Nuvoletta clan of Camorra, and the Sacra Corona Unita (in the Apulia region). It had employed computer experts to run spear-phishing emails that duped victims into sending money to bank accounts, which they pilfered and then laundered through front companies, money mules, and cryptocurrency assets. When the operation was dismantled, the authorities discovered that the intergang operations led to the formation of a pyramid structure, which included different specialized roles similar to the ones characterizing the Mariposa and GozNym cliques.

The code name used by the authorities for taking down the organization was, as mentioned, Fontana-Almabahía; it involved 106 arrests, many on the Spanish island of Tenerife (Vavra, 2021). The Italian mafiosi brought their tried-and-true tactics of coercive money laundering schemes to the online medium, where they were greatly amplified. Significantly, the arrested persons were also accused of land-based crimes, such as kidnapping, assault, robbery with violence, illegal possession of weapons, and homicide. Given the implications of this case, it will be revisited in more detail in the final chapter. As criminologist Federico Varese remarked after the arrests were made (cited in Vavra, 2021):

> This kind of overlap between cybercrime and physical violations of the law is more common than you might think. There is a common misconception about cybercrime that it only happens online. Instead, there's an important, offline dimension, where people with some cyber expertise meet traditional organized crime. Everything I've seen points to a very clear division of labor. The traditional mafia – they would be divorced.

Case Study: Operation Trojan Shield

As discussed in the previous chapter, one of the most important take down operations in cybercrime history was called Trojan Shield (United States Southern District of California, Case Number: '21 CR1623 JLS). Hundreds of arrests were made in Australia and across Europe. The joint police operation was made possible by a covert use of the FBI's encrypted device application called Anom. Undercover agents sold the application, as a secure device, to more than 300 criminal syndicates in more than 100 countries. The users unknowingly promoted the application and communicated daily with it, allowing agents to monitor and catalogue more than 27 million messages between users. They openly discussed narcotics concealment methods, shipments, money laundering, and violent threats. The messages also revealed how the drugs would be moved about in the real world, such as concealing cocaine in loads of pineapples, bananas, and even cans of tuna, to elude law enforcement's detection.

This case brings out a form of Machiavellian irony, which the Italian philosopher expressed as follows – the best way to defeat the deceivers is by deception (paraphrased from Machiavelli's *The Prince*, 1513). Because encrypted devices provide a shield against surveillance and detection, the irony here is that the same type of device that the criminals used to hide from the law was used against them. The Operation also highlighted the emergence of a new kind of sting operation involving technologies. Trojan Shield arose, in effect, "because of a grand dupe" (Kampmark, 2021). The FBI had recruited an informant to develop an adulterated version of the encryption technology platform Anom, used on modified cell phones for distribution throughout the organized crime network. It included a calculator app which relayed all communications back to the FBI. As Kampmark (2021) remarked, the case opened a whole new way of "fighting crime with crime," which has implications for the future of criminal investigations (as will be discussed in the final chapter):

> While the criminals in question might well have been mocked for their gullibility, the trumpeting of law enforcement did not seem much better. A relentless campaign has been waged on end-to-end encryption communication platforms, a war against what policing types call "going dark." To add some light to the situation, the agencies pine for the creation of tailored backdoors to such communications apps as WhatsApp, iMessage, and Signal.

Epilogue

The use of digital technologies to communicate, plan crimes, seek victims, negotiate drug deals, and the like through cyberspace, and then carry out the physical components of the crimes in the real world, is at the core of hybrid criminality. Because it involves cooperation among different and even disparate criminal organizations, as well as the recruitment of technically skilled individuals, hybrid criminality has changed the nature of organized crime, amplifying its reach considerably in new and historically anomalous ways. As the United Nations Office on Drugs and Crime (2018) has pointed out, organized crime now falls under three rubrics: it can be "cyber-assisted," which means that it simply uses the new technologies as ancillary tools; it can be "cyber-enabled," whereby long-standing forms of organized crime, such as illicit gambling, fraud, and extortion, are given a global reach through technologies; or it can be "cyber-dependent," involving malware and ransomware, and which thus depends on the Internet.

As our sources emphasized, the new generation of mafiosi has been reared in the age of the matrix. As a result, they have few emotional ties to the past and its archaic value systems and strictly defined behaviors. As the world has become increasingly interconnected via technology, it is only natural that organized crime has had to adapt. The use of sophisticated information systems is no longer solely the realm of the hacker and the coder; it is now also the realm of drug dealer, extortionist, and illegal gambler. Currency is no longer sponsored solely by governments but also by digital groups. Internet provides a sense of anonymity to users. Anonymity, in turn, spawns vice, luring organized criminals, who are only too happy to capitalize on it. Cases such as the Anom one have become somewhat routine. In July 2020, for instance, the EncroChat-encrypted platform was dismantled by the Operational Taskforce EMMA (France, the Netherlands), which alarmed criminal organizations across Europe; it was followed in 2021 with another similar takedown by a joint police operation in Belgium, France, and the Netherlands, who successfully blocked the use of encrypted communications by organized crime networks. McLuhan's amplification notion is clearly operative in hybrid criminality. Illegal drugs are now shipped via global transportation networks. Money laundering can be carried out more broadly. Criminal cultures are no longer limited to having their base in their countries of origin, finding new locales in cyberspace. But this is a two-edged sword for criminal organizations. For one, the authorities now use the same tools to take them down. For another, they become ever-more dependent on technology, and thus risk disintegrating into anonymous criminal "hubs." The claim to distinctiveness is thus in peril. Traditional mafias lived in a "gray" zone, establishing connections with those in power; today, the gray zone has turned into a dark one, based on links among each other in the dark regions of cyberspace. And while they cling to their archaic symbolism and rites, they have had to rebrand themselves through social media platforms (Chapter 5). The Internet has also given rise to neo-gangs that form in cyberspace, adding to the sense of obsolescence associated with previous organized criminality. Moreover, it has generated a dualistic criminal persona (to be discussed further in Chapter 4), which inhabits the Dark Web for the conduct of its illegal operations and the public world of social media for purposes of vanity and everyday communications. As far back as 2010, the fugitive 'Ndrangheta boss and one of the 100 most wanted Italian criminals, Pasquale Manfredi, was tracked down through his Facebook account, registered under the handle of Scarface – the famous nickname of Al Capone, which he had ostentatiously adopted for himself. The irony is that Manfredi was caught because of his use of social media. Even Sammy "The Bull" Gravano – the iconic, ruthless hitman for New York's Gambino crime family – posted regularly on Instagram and TikTok, as well as hosting his own podcast, garnering millions of views for his YouTube videos in which he revisits his past with stories about taking hostages, murdering people, and disposing of bodies – crimes for which he was convicted and sent to prison for 20 years. Gravano is an Internet mobster celebrity, collecting money for his viral videos and selling lots of merchandise.

But all this does not mean that organized crime syndicates are giving up their old, violent ways – as our police sources emphasized. They still settle debts brutally, engage in offline extortion and fraud, and so on. The older clan members are actually suspicious of the new cryptocurrencies. As one of our sources stated, a typical mafioso would think: "How do I know I am not being cheated with all these new things?" This rhetorical question encapsulates the dilemma in which mafia-type organizations now find themselves. Nonetheless, the move from gray to dark regions has been inevitable and highly profitable. There is no staying away from the world of the matrix – a universe where traditional barriers collapse, and traditional mafias are fragmented. Carmen Hermosillo's notion of "self-congratulation" in the world of matrix certainly applies to Gravano, Manfredi, and many others (cited in Curtis, 2011):

> So-called electronic communities encourage participation in fragmented, mostly silent, micro-groups who are primarily engaged in dialogues of self-congratulation. In other words, most people lurk; and the ones that post are pleased with themselves.

As one of the creators of *Matrix* movie, Andy Wachowski (2012) aptly observed, we are constantly involved in a tiresome construction of meaning – a process that mafiosi have also not been able to avoid:

> What we were trying to achieve with the story overall was a shift, the same kind of shift that happens for Neo, that Neo goes from being in this sort of cocooned and programmed world, to having to participate in the construction of meaning to his life.

3

DARK MAFIA

Prologue

The elusive and ever-morphing figure of the mobster in popular culture as a handsome and charming young man, yet brutal killer – all wrapped into one – is a nostalgic trope generated initially by Hollywood and continuing as a stereotypical image in the Internet Age in contemporary movies and even videogames. This is, however, an archaic image; the contemporary mafioso is on his way to becoming a tech-savvy plotter, increasingly involved in crimes planned and committed in the darkest regions of cyberspace, but who appears on social media platforms to present himself ostentatiously to the general public. As an inhabitant of the dark regions, hidden from view, the mafioso operates secretively as a "dark mobster", at the same time that, as an inhabitant of the social media universe, he basks in vanity, displaying his riches, tattoos, and extravagant lifestyle for everyone to see – reflecting the dualistic character of the Mafia 2.0. Moreover, given the hybrid nature of organized crime, real-world operations and online schemes conducted on the Dark Web are no longer separate forms of criminality; they are coordinated ones, as Europol's *Serious and Organised Crime Threat Assessment* (2018) has emphasized.

Today, ransomware, DDoS attacks, and other cybercriminal schemes bring vast amounts of money to criminal organizations, largely replacing (or at least reinforcing) their previous protection

DOI: 10.4324/9781003278597-4

money and extortion schemes. Through the Dark Web, also known as the Dark Net (despite differences), organized criminals can now easily blackmail individuals, steal their money anonymously via phishing and social engineering scams, threaten victims without having to use physical force, while remaining anonymous. Operations such as the Black Hand threats of the 1920s, which involved sending threats by handwritten letters to select victims, pale in comparison to the reach that cyberspace permits. The Black Hand has become the Dark Hand, terrorizing and extorting countless victims in many ways. As journalist Jamie Bartlett (2016) has argued in his book, *The Dark Net*, cyberspace is hardly a brave new world, paraphrasing Aldous Huxley, but a terrifying one that generally has profound implications for society, especially given the opportunities it affords to criminals. The Dark Web is where illegal marketplaces have emerged to facilitate and significantly expand the conduct of traditional criminal operations – drug sales in these venues, for instance, attract buyers and sellers from anywhere on the globe. It is on such dark ground that criminal partnerships are now forged, even though criminals may have never even met each other in person nor know each other's real-world identities. As discussed, the Silk Road site was the first highly profitable dark marketplace (Chapter 1), whose owner and operator, Ross Ulbricht, earned millions of dollars illegally, expending little effort to do so (U.S. v. Ulbricht 2014, 2017). It inspired countless subsequent marketplaces that aimed to follow its basic model of operations, including Dream Market, founded in late 2013 by Gal Vallerius (U.S. v. Vallerius 2018:*1), which allowed online users to browse it anonymously. It sold drugs, stolen data, and counterfeit consumer goods with cryptocurrency, bringing Vallerius a veritable fortune until it was shut down in 2019.

The advent of dark marketplaces has also led to the rise to new forms of investigation, as discussed with regard to the Trojan Horse Shield case (Chapter 1). In that operation, the authorities utilized or developed digital technologies themselves while forging international partnership to confront transnational criminality in a coordinated fashion. A well-known case of the latter is the 2016 one, called Operation Hyperion, which involved the cooperation of enforcement agencies in the United States, Australia, Canada, New Zealand, the United Kingdom, and Europol. They utilized an online version of the "knock and talk" technique, whereby police investigators "knocked" on the virtual door of the Dark Web portals, aiming to identify buyers and sellers. The case also showed that real-world operations could be synchronized with the virtual part of the investigation. The use of regular mail finally led to the arrest of the online operators since the buyers had the illegal packages delivered directly to their houses, in their names. Intercepting the packages allowed the investigators to trace where exactly they came from. However, the criminal organization quickly learned from this mistake and started using drones and other ways to make deliveries, avoiding the kind of trap set by Operation Hyperion. Simultaneously, the drone method eliminated the need for mules and other couriers in other situations.

Despite law enforcement successes, hybrid criminality, based in dark marketplaces, has significantly strengthened criminal operations, expanding their reach worldwide with the simple click of a mouse or touch of a screen. As McLuhan had anticipated, before the Internet came into being, the global system of interconnectedness that digital–electronic technologies make possible, implies that previously disparate gangs would see the benefit of pooling resources and synchronizing activities. The locus for these is the Dark Web.

The Dark Web

The Internet enfolds World Wide Web content via overlay systems that can be accessed through specific software or configurations (Bartlett, 2016). The Dark Web, in contrast, forms a section on the so-called Deep Web – the region of the Web that is not indexed by regular search engines, containing a vast network of sites and communities where the liberty to do whatever anyone wants is pushed to its limits. The Dark Web actually has many legal websites, including peer-to-peer platforms and networks such as Freenet, which are operated by legitimate organizations and individuals. Users of these sites refer to the regular Internet as the "clearnet," and to the Dark Web as the "darknet" (written as one word). Although there is a technical distinction between Dark Net and Dark Web, the two are often used as synonyms. The Dark Web has allowed traditional organized crime groups to interact with each other profitably, alongside new criminal actors such as hackers, stalkers, political extremists, bitcoin scammers, vigilantes, and hitmen-for-hire.

As early studies showed (i.e., United Nations Office on Drugs and Crime, 2013), some of the real-world organized crime's traditional operations and schemes cannot be adapted easily to cyberspace. An example is that of territorial control – a mainstay feature of traditional mafia operations (United Nations Office on Drugs and Crime, 2013: 45). As Varese (2010: 14) observed, this led to new ways to "regulate and control the production and distribution of a given commodity or service unlawfully." The task fell to the new online administrators who would monitor sites and content to ensure that platform's rules were enforced – excluding noncompliance groups from the site. Already during this early stage of online coordination, several problems emerged. One of these involved figuring out ways of distributing or delivering the goods in real space, which posed a serious problem to the dealers, as Operation Hyperion showed. Another issue concerned the delivery location, since it could be anywhere on the planet, unlike the designated territories of the past according to clan. Deliveries would have to be coordinated transnationally and individuals hired anywhere in the world to carry them out. Yet another problem was the following one: while the production and distribution of a given illegal commodity are controlled in darknet sites, they do not extend to other online forums, thus limiting the reach and operationality of the dark networks (Leukfeldt et al., 2017: 296). As a result, when the dark marketplace sites are dismantled by law enforcement, the network associated with them ceases to exist as well, with exceptions, such as when the members who have escaped apprehension have created another site that mirrors the one taken down. The classic case in point is the Silk Road 2.0, which mimicked the original Silk Road site to preserve its operational continuity (Maras, 2016).

Another emerging problem regarded the migration to cyberspace itself and the need to coordinate Internet and Dark Web operations. The solution was an obvious one: Internet technologies would be used to communicate routinely; Dark Web technologies would be used instead to plan and coordinate operations in secrecy. But this produced an anomaly in the structural constitution and identity of organized crime groups. The dark marketplaces allow them to commit an enormous range of crimes, hidden from the sight of the public and the authorities. The problem is that after an operation has been realized, many of the actors, such as money mules, hackers, and others, disappear or go on to work for other criminal entities, thus making the overall operationality of a criminal organization tenuous during transition periods. Moreover, the Internet itself presents its own set of problems. Used to forge and sustain a public image, it exposes mobsters considerably, as some of the case studies discussed previously in this book have shown. Yet, despite these problems, from the outset, it was clear that the migration to cyberspace had become a necessity, despite the problems. As the early United Nations Office on Drugs and Crime (2013) report concluded, these problems emerged because of the migration itself to cyberspace by organized criminal groups who "tend to exist on a continuum between ephemeral and sustainable with hybrids in the middle and use Internet technologies to organize themselves to a lesser or greater extent."

To reiterate, the Dark Web is the region of the Web that is not mapped to search engines such as Google; it is accessible only through specialized browsers, utilizing non-recognizable web addresses that are readable only by those browsers. The surface Web is actually much smaller than the Dark Web, making up less than 10 percent of World Wide Web content. As mentioned, there are legitimate aspects of the Dark Web, which having nothing to do with criminality, including email accounts, social networking sites, cloud service accounts, online banking, education sites, video on demand, digital magazines, data shared on private social networks, and so on. But it is the dark marketplaces controlled by criminals that pose great problems to both the authorities and the public at large, as early ones like Silk Road made obvious to everyone. It was one of the first marketplaces that allowed users to browse anonymously and securely. At first, the new sellers had to purchase an account via an auction; later, a fixed fee was charged for each new account. In November 2020, the U.S. government seized more than one billion dollars' worth of bitcoin connected to the Silk Road operations, describing it as a model of hybrid criminality. The indictment underlined the extensiveness of the operations involved.

As Interpol (2021) emphasized after a large scale investigation, dark marketplaces have extended the reach of illegal operations worldwide, making it much harder to investigate crimes, including everything from drug dealing, extortion, and credit scams to human trafficking. As the report notes, any crime can now be planned online and then executed via covert transactions in real space. The Dark Web has, in effect, made it possible for mobsters to perpetrate crimes at a distance, in virtual anonymity, and with a worldwide reach. The significance of dark markets for organized crime was emphasized early on by Misha Glenny in his 2011 book, *DarkMarket: Cyberthieves, Cybercops and You*, in which he explains how cybercriminal networks have opened up opportunities that were unthinkable in the past – all made possible by the world of the matrix.

The Dark Marketplace

In 2021, law enforcement took down one of the largest Dark Web illegal marketplaces since the Silk Road, called DarkMarket, which was founded in 2019. It hosted 20 servers, allowing buyers and sellers to negotiate within an entrepreneurial, peer-reviewed environment. The police operation involved agencies in Germany, Australia, Denmark, Moldova, Ukraine, the United Kingdom, and the United States – which were assisted by Europol's own specialized operational analysis. The DarkMarket figures are remarkable – it had almost 500,000 users; more than 2,400 sellers; over 320,000 transactions; around 4,650 bitcoin and 13,000 monero transfers, corresponding to nearly 150 billion euros. Its main activities were illegal drugs, counterfeit money, stolen or fake credit cards, anonymous SIM cards, and the sale of malware. As this case emphasized, dark marketplaces are huge criminal enterprises, rivaling the profits made by the largest legitimate corporations and certainly exceeding the financial gains that the real-world mafias could only have imagined. There is little doubt that this lucrative aspect of hybrid criminality was critical in convincing traditional mafias to move some of their operational bases online. At the same time, dark mafias have had to develop new ways of avoiding detection and capture, given the emergence of highly sophisticated coordinated police operations, as the DarkMarket takedown operation showed.

A year after this operation, police forces in nine countries pooled their resources to arrest 150 suspects involved in buying or selling illicit goods on the Dark Web. Called Dark HunTOR, the police operation netted millions of euros in cash, virtual currencies, drugs, and firearms, involving investigators from Australia, Bulgaria, France, Germany, Italy, the Netherlands, Switzerland, the United Kingdom, and the United States. Due to such successful operations, Europol has set up a Joint Cybercrime Action Taskforce (2022), which it hosts at its headquarters in The Hague, the Netherlands, to help coordinate transnational police investigations.

Despite such dramatic takedowns, the profitability of the dark marketplaces continues to be a significant incentive for mafia-type organizations to engage in hybrid criminality, especially since it has allowed them to open up new vast territories to carry out their traditional and new activities (Décary-Hétu and Dupont, 2013). Because of ever-increasing computer power and versatility, criminals can now easily send large amounts of spam for fraudulent purposes, attack web servers for ransom or blackmail money, or steal financial data – through an everyday computer screen in front of them. This has introduced the figure of the "botmaster" into organized crime, whose computer and network expertise places him high up in the hierarchy of criminal hybrid structure. The botmaster can build and tailor botnets to meet the demands of the criminals, which are then used for creating computer worms, detecting software vulnerabilities of designated victims, and tricking victims into installing software that will allow criminals to remotely control a computer (Décary-Hétu and Dupont, 2013: 177).

Overall, the dark marketplaces offer many kinds of advantages to mobsters, allowing them to facilitate and expand operations, at the same time that they can carry out transactions with other criminals across the globe. But this new world of criminality has introduced new kinds of problems, as already discussed, for the criminals, including the danger that the money and data that the marketplace processes can be stolen by a clever third party operating outside of the criminal organization. However, as discussed, the greatest danger to mobsters is that the authorities are becoming increasingly capable of entering the marketplaces undetected, carrying out sting operations and other entrapment strategies and, of course, benefiting from human error. Even though victims are at the mercy of criminals, since identifying the scammers is not easy to do, sooner or later, missteps are taken that will rebound on the criminals who, when arrested, are impelled by law to provide some sort of reparation.

One other problem that cyberspace presents to criminals is that it has constrained their ability to respond to insults and denigrations. In the offline world, these were met with a quick and brutal vindictive response, to uphold the honor code of the clan. When honor is impugned, a mobster is seen as morally spineless unless he enacts a revenge scheme to regain his reputation. It is difficult to envision how a mafioso can respond to virtual insults, given that it is often impossible to identify the insulter. Does this mean that mobsters may have to adapt in this domain as well? Is the concept of honor fading, given the difficulty of defending it in cyberspace? Or is it still firmly embedded in mafia culture but more elusive to defend and even unstable? The traditional criminal organizations are "cultures of honor." No better code illustrates this than *omertà*, espoused by the Italian mafias, which envisions honor as based in humble obedient behavior and a pledge of loyalty to the crime family. Do the following words of the late mafioso Antonino Calderone, a leading figure of the Sicilian Mafia in the 1970s, still apply (cited in Follain, 2009: 25)?

> You must forgive me for this distinction I make between the Mafia and common crime, but it's important to me. It's important to every Mafioso. We are Mafiosi, the others are just the rabble. We are men of honour. And not so much because we have sworn an oath, but because we are the elite of crime. We are very much superior to common criminals. We are the worst of all!

Of course, obedience to the clan is still a part of organized crime – but this does not mean that it denotes what it did in the past, given the new types of tech leaders who are involved in the organization by necessity. There is no code of honor as such in cyberspace, just a code of convenient relationships. The traditional code of omertà produced a shared sense of invulnerability and personal empowerment, providing members with the impetus to take extraordinary risks, and allowing them to rationalize their criminal behavior. No such sense is required in organized cybercrime. There is no "empathy of belonging," based on an honor code, in the vastness of cyberspace, where everything is in constant flux, and obsolescence a constant pattern. Because cybercriminality is now a fact of life for the mafiosi, the traditions based on historically and geographically shaped codes of honor are evanescing in the ether of cyberspace (Chapter 4). Are the new generations of mafiosi still adherent to the traditional codes, or are they adapting them idiosyncratically to the world of the matrix? As journalist Oisin Sweeney (2021) has argued, this world may have obliterated the historical forces that have always been at work in preserving criminal cultures, as the latest generations of criminals bring a new unhistorical mindset to their illegal activities. They have grown up in front of the computer screen, satisfying their hunger for power in more public ways, which would have been deemed unwise and even foolish in the past. This does not imply, however, that the young mafiosi do not want to exert the same kind of power over people as did their predecessors. As Sweeney (2021) notes, "Many [mafia groups] have now begun using social media to bolster their image, in a move that criminologists note is an efficient way to remind locals of their dominance without resorting to violence."

The case of Vincenzo Torcasio can be recalled here as a case in point (Chapter 2). His posts on social media showed that he reveled in the ability that the computer screen afforded him to show off his extravagant lifestyle; it also allowed him to threaten rivals or victims through menacing images and posts of all kinds. His case has become a norm, as criminal organizations use social media regularly, not only for branding and self-promotion purposes but also to remind people of their wealth and power. Torcasio's communications on Facebook also showed that the code of silence in public no longer applies, at least in the same way. This does not mean that trust and loyalty have disappeared as part of the mafioso's value system; it means that they have taken on new forms. As Maras (2016: 344) has pointed out, criminals in dark marketplaces still rely on the establishment of rules of enforcement and agreements of trust which is

> critical when relying on others in high risk and vulnerable situations to deliver goods and services, especially when the transactions are illicit in nature. Victims of non-delivery or counterfeit items cannot report this to the police, because they have engaged in unlawful conduct.

Mafia-type organizations have always engaged in "black markets;" so in a way, the online "dark markets" can be conceived to be McLuhanian extensions of these, having amplified their range of operations considerably. What makes dark markets more threatening and powerful is that they are geographically spread out, diverse, and anonymous. As a study by Norgaard et al. (2018: 877) has argued, their network structure has made it obvious to the older clans that they have no choice but to abandon their traditional codes and forms of hierarchical structure:

> Traditional black markets are relatively hierarchical, with high degree and high betweenness. We compare the density and average length of the shortest path of the simulated Ground black market networks with our simulated Virtual network. We find that hierarchy and monopolization tendencies in networks are products of different transaction costs and information asymmetries. The Internet is an effective way to lower multiple aspects of network structure. We observe that the network structure surrounding the interactions in the Virtual black

market is less hierarchical and slightly more monopolistic than the network structure of the Ground market.

Dark Language

Criminal organizations have constantly developed modes of secret communication, including (a) the use of dialectal forms of a language (*in-group code*), as exemplified by the communicative practices of the Italian mafias; (b) encrypted messaging (*secretive code*), which allows them to hide their intentions from public and police scrutiny; and (c) the use of a style intended to intimidate victims, either explicitly or by innuendo, exploiting their fears (*threatening code*). These codes can be categorized under the general rubric of "dark language," a language that resonates linguistically and operationally with the dark market criminal economy.

The classic example of an *in-group code* pertains to the use of original dialects by the Italian mafias, who typically use older regional forms of Sicilian, Neapolitan, or Calabrian, or other dialects (Nicaso and Danesi, 2021). This has allowed organized criminals to connect themselves to the history of the regions in which they operate, legitimizing themselves through the channel of the "real" historical languages of their regions. Secretive codes are found throughout organized criminality. The use of cryptography, for instance, has been adopted by members of criminal organizations to communicate with each other in secret code so that they can avoid the decipherment of message interceptions and even eavesdropping on the part of the authorities. A well-known example goes back to 2006, when police found the encrypted notes of a Sicilian Mafia boss, Bernardo Provenzano, during the execution of a warrant. These were easily decoded, however, leading to his arrest after years on the run and also giving investigators crucial information for tracking down other clan members since the notes contained orders from Provenzano to his lieutenants. In another classic case, Italian police decrypted a document of the Calabrian 'Ndrangheta in 2016 written in a strange code resembling the use of various alphabet-based ciphers – Greek, Cyrillic, and Egyptian. After it was decoded, the document provided relevant information about a secret initiation oath that recruits had to recite before becoming full-fledged members of the clan (Nicaso and Danesi, 2021).

Such cases bring out a well-known point about organized criminal groups. They use secret codes much like military organizations do to communicate with each other confidentially. Secret writing lets the members keep outsiders out and insiders relatively free of prying investigative eyes. This use of cryptography is, in fact, a pseudo-military one, indicating that organized criminals see themselves as an army with a military structure. In dark marketplaces, the cryptographic element is central to criminal operations. The ability to create and use encrypted information is critical for the conduct of these sites. Not correctly encrypting the information in transit, use, or storage opens up huge vulnerabilities for the criminal organization. For protection against decryption, such sites use an algorithm's random encryption key, making it virtually impenetrable. But this has not deterred the authorities. Recall the Anom sting operation as a case in point, which involved an app that allowed the FBI to monitor criminal communications as they were transmitted, which they used for their indictments.

Intimidating language (*threatening code*) has been a part of criminal behavior from time immemorial. Even though it does not relate to organized crime, one of the classic cases of such language concerns a note written by David Berkowitz, the Son of Sam serial killer, found in a car upon his arrest on August 10, 1977 (Gibson, 2004). Even before reading the note's message, several features immediately stand out. First, Berkowitz used only capital block letters, suggesting fear. The leftward slant to the top of the letters "T" and "I" followed the overall leftward slant of the writing, likely indicating an unconscious leaning toward the "sinister" (from Latin meaning "left") – a hunch reinforced by the occult and ominous contents of the note, as can be seen in phrases such as "The duke of death," "The wicked king of wicker," "the twenty-two disciples of hell," and "rapist and suffocator of young girls." As the police eventually found out, the name "Sam" was a reference to Berkowitz's neighbor, Sam Carr, who Berkowitz believed was a demon, claiming that Carr's black Labrador retriever passed on to him the dark commands that motivated him to kill. Significantly, Berkowitz himself, under interrogation, referred to his handwriting style as intended to produce a "ghoulish effect," matching his demonic fantasies and apprehensions in a stylistic way. The Berkowitz note is an example of what has been called "dark language" here. Its intent is to convey fear to its readers, at the same time that it reveals the mindset of the writer.

As Interpol (2021) has documented, this type of language is common online, as criminals send threatening messages to their victims in the same kind of style used by Berkowitz. However, it also leaves a stylistic fingerprint which can be used by the authorities in Dark Web investigations since it could potentially offer indications on the users' profiles and origins. After running a Dark Web crawler on Nigerian gangs, Interpol (2021) found that, in addition to English, French, and Portuguese, local African languages and dialects were used by the Nigerian criminals to enhance the fear factor, recalling the use of dialects on the part of Italian mobsters. The Nigerian scammers often worked from scripts of prewritten American English – standardized pieces of text for use as clauses in communications – to which they subsequently added threatening words when the victim was noncompliant.

Another aspect of dark language is the use of new visual writing forms, such as emojis, which have been appearing more frequently since at least 2015. They have become part of an ever-expanding visual lexicon of aggression used by gangs for enhancing threats or for self-serving purposes. For example, the Bloods and Crips use emojis as part of a secret in-group code not only to plan crimes, but also to mock their rivals or threaten their victims. The Harlem Crips use the two-thumbs-up emoji, with the knuckles facing each other, as an identity symbol. At the same time, the rival Bloods show their gang affiliation symbolism with a magician's top hat emoji. Showing disrespect for such symbols by posting them upside down has led to various conflicts. As William Wan (2018) has remarked:

> Instead of tagging graffiti, some rival gang members now upload video of themselves chanting slurs in enemy territory. Taunts and fights that once played out over time on the street are these days hurled instantaneously on Twitter and Instagram. The online aggression can quickly translate into outbreaks of real violence – teens killing each other over emoji and virtually relayed gang signs. Social media have profoundly changed gang activity in the United States. Of particular concern, researchers say, is how social media often appear to amplify and speed up the cycle of aggression and violence.

In reviewing materials provided by law enforcement agencies in various countries, we found that emoji use among younger members of criminal organizations is common. Often, the emojis are veiled threats, such as a smiley accompanying a verbal statement. We also found chain emojis to represent a prison and the syringe with blood emoji to express brotherhood. Additionally, we found emoji lions, crowns, and bombs as symbols of strength and courage on various gang websites and platforms. Hashtags were included for various symbolic reasons, such as the hashtag #ES17, created in homage to Emanuele Sibillo, a camorrista killed by a rival gang in 2015 at nineteen years of age.

A Digital Black Hand

An example of a dark language style to intimidate victims goes back to the early twentieth century in the United States, when so-called *Mano Nera* ("Black Hand") gangs emerged as extortion groups. The victims were members of Italian immigrant communities, who would receive a letter warning them to give the sender a certain sum of money or else risk death at the hands of a secret "Black Hand Society." The letters were often signed distinctively with a black handprint as a visual enhancement of the fear factor.

The most infamous Black Hander was an immigrant from Sicily named Ignazio Saietta, also known as "Lupo the Wolf." Saietta lived with his brother-in-law Nicholas Morello, who had built a small criminal empire in New York City. He joined his brother-in-law's gang but also carried out his Black Hand operations separately, exploiting the innate distrust of authority among the Sicilian immigrants who owned businesses into a self-serving racket. The subtext of the messages was: "Pay this or die." In 1908, there were over 400 documented cases of Black Hand extortion in New York City. Between 1910 and 1914, over 100 murders were attributed to the Black Hand. Due to a similarity in extortion methods, the police at the time believed that Black Handers were closely aligned with the Sicilian Mafia. However, no verifiable links were found, nor was a large centralized Black Hand gang operation ever discovered. What is particularly interesting here is the Black Hand style of intimidation. The following are examples of Black Hand letters, found in Morello's home by William Flynn of the Secret Service:

Mr. Battaglia: Do not think that we are dead. Look out for your face; a veil won't help you. Now is the occasion to give me five hundred dollars on account of that which you others don't know respect that from then to now you should have kissed my forehead I have been in your store, friend. Donate how you respect him he is an ignorant boob, that I bring you others I hope that all will end that when we are alone they give me no peace as I deserve time lost that brings you will know us neither some other of the Mafia in the future will write in the bank where you must send the money without so many stories otherwise you will pay for it.

Dear Friend: Beware we are sick and tired of writing to you to the appointment you have not come with people of honor. If this time you don't do what we say it will be your ruination. Send us three hundred dollars with people of honor at eleven o'clock Thursday night. There will be a friend at the corner of 15th Street and Hamilton Ave. He will ask you for the signal. Give me the word and you will give him the money. Beware that if you don't come to this order we will ruin all your merchandise and attempt your life. Beware of what you do. M. N. [Mano Nera]

Friend: The need obliges us to come to you in order to do us a favor. We request, Sunday night, 7th day, at 12 o'clock you must bring the sum of $1000. Under penalty of death for you and your dears you must come under the new bridge near the Grand Street ferry where you will find the person that wants to know the time. At this word you will give him the money. Beware of what you do and keep your mouth shut.

The Black Hand episode left residues of stereotypical views of Italian immigrant communities for a considerable period of time. In 1911, American wildlife artist Charles Robert Knight protested against the use of the term Black Hand as an example of discrimination targeting the Italian community as a whole in a letter he wrote to the *Chicago Record-Herald*. Knight cited the case of Joseph Vacek, who, after having killed his father, left a note at the crime scene signed "Mano Nera." After Vacek confessed to the truth, his ruse showed that the term Black Hand was indeed being used to scapegoat a certain group – the Italian communities in the U.S.

Although not named as such, the Black Hand style has gone digital. In 2018, the National Directorate of Intelligence and Customs Investigations of the French police shut down one of the largest illegal Dark Web marketplaces, calling itself the "Black Hand," which was selling drugs, weapons, databases, stolen banking data, and fake documents. After gaining access to the server, authorities also seized falsified documents, 4,000 euros, virtual currencies, and computer equipment. A few days later, the French police arrested a vendor, OxyMonster, on the Dark Web, who pleaded guilty to selling drugs. The communications recovered via posts and other messaging services included messages that imitated the original Black Hand ones, used when the victims failed to comply with a phishing scam.

In legends, frightening dark mythical creatures came out at night. They are imaginary manifestations of what Carl Jung (1971: 12) called the Shadow archetype. The psychological effect of Black Hand tactics may well be traced to the unconscious fears associated with this archetype. In the past, the dark bogeyman was a figment of the imagination; today, he is real and living in the Internet's darkest corners.

Case Studies: III

As mentioned several times, in 2013, the Silk Road emerged as a Dark Web marketplace that was imitated broadly after its takedown. Such marketplaces have, in fact, spread throughout the Dark Web, posing an increasing danger to regular economies. The case studies here show how such markets are established and spread. To cite Misha Glenny (2018), cases such as these reveal that the world of hybrid organized crime has truly changed the nature of criminality, which now uses the Dark Web to plan online and offline activities to great advantage:

> As the fusion between traditional organized crime and cybercrime proceeds, the structure of cybercriminal groups has assumed the hierarchies usually associated with its real-life counterpart. The days of the script kiddies, those mischief-making 15-year-olds bombing your computer with viruses, are over. Now cybercriminals have a boss and a council who are making decisions, a coding and malware department, a social engineering department, a finance department and then an army of foot soldiers responsible for laundering the money.

Case Study: Ramnicu Valcea

As the Silk Road case showed, cyberspace has allowed random criminal groups to arise online without any ties to previous criminal organizations. One of the first such cases is a hub that was constituted in Ramnicu Valcea at the turn of the Millennium, a town in the mountains of Romania, which subsequently came to be known as Hackerville. The hub was formed when the depressed job market in Romania at the time motivated a group of individuals with computer skills to turn to crime so as to be able to make money via hacking and fraud schemes. By 2002, the group's operations became widespread, with the criminals using Internet cafes to post fake ads on eBay for products they did not own, having the money wire-transferred to the criminal organization by their victims. To avoid detection, the hackers created legitimate-looking websites that advertised products such as automobiles at meager prices, posing as American soldiers stationed overseas whose cars were in storage back home and needed to be sold. They would ask for an advance payment for the nonexistent vehicles, but when word caught on about the scam operation, the hackers changed their approach, asking for no payment except shipping costs. The security company Norton labeled Ramnicu Valcea as "the most dangerous town on the Internet," having established a self-made digital operation which reached around the world (Moran et al., 2019). The Rumanian hackers operated what is arguably the first Dark Web marketplace, even before the arrival of the Web 2.0 world. It showed that criminals are among the first to understand and take advantage of emerging technologies, well ahead of the authorities.

One of the hackers, Marcel Lazar Lehel, known as Guccifer, was arrested in 2014 on charges of hacking prominent U.S. officials and their families. Interestingly, he initially had no particular computer expertise or access to sophisticated equipment. He learned what to purchase and how to use it from the Web itself. Given its notoriety, the hub even became the inspiration in 2019 of the HBO series, *Hackerville*, which revolved around the activities of a gifted adolescent hacker who was pursued by the police and by those who wanted to exploit his skill, after he broke into a bank with simple computer skills.

As this case showed, the opportunities that cyberspace offers to start-up criminal organizations are limitless, a fact corroborated by many subsequent cases, such as one involving three men on

Vancouver Island in Canada, running a cryptocurrency-funded online drug trafficking ring, called AlwaysOverweight. In early 2019, the Federal Serious and Organized Crime section of the Royal Canadian Mounted Police (2022) initiated a successful online undercover investigation into the crime group, identifying its operators. All of them had only basic computer skills that they used to carry out their schemes, including the trafficking of a large variety of drugs such as methamphetamine, oxycodone, cocaine, Xanax, and fentanyl. The group used cryptocurrency and encrypted messaging applications that allowed it to flourish in anonymity and organize itself strategically online for a while. The RCMP's complex online investigation allowed the agents to locate the street-level drug transactions, leading them to three suspects living in Nanaimo, British Columbia, where they were arrested on February 4, 2020. Search warrants led to the discovery of drugs, digital documents, cash, computers, and data storage devices.

Case Study: Operation Uptick

The changes that the Internet brought about at the turn of the Millennium, making cases such as the ones above common, did not escape the attention of traditional organized crime. In 2000, over 600 FBI agents arrested and charged 120 people with securities fraud, uncovering a broad scheme that combined old-style mob violence and bribery with new emerging digital investment strategies (Walsh, 2000). The operation, known as Uptick, targeted the five families of Cosa Nostra in New York City, and in particular the Bonanno and the Colombo families, whose members set up a so-called DMN Capital Investments Inc. firm that provided purported investment banking services to small, developing companies. DMN had no legal status and was used only as a cover for reasons of fraud. This case is a starting point for the emergence of hybrid criminality among traditional organized crime. The charges ranged from racketeering and securities fraud to solicitation of murder, money laundering, and extortion, involving not only mobsters themselves but also money managers, brokers, lawyers, pension fund officials, and even a New York City police detective.

Operation Uptick had begun a year earlier, involving confidential informants and a court-ordered bug in the office of DMN Capital Investments, with the FBI recording more than 1,000 hours of conversations. Several websites were named in the indictment, showing how mobsters had coordinated their efforts to fraudulently tout certain stocks – called "micro-caps" – raising their value by sending out bulk messages and emails. The case was a model of how hybrid criminality would evolve. Members of the American Cosa Nostra had clearly understood that cyberspace offered new possibilities for carrying out fraudulent activities and moving money around anonymously.

One of our sources pointed out that such cases are now common in Europe, with criminal organizations offering fraudulent offshore financial services, anonymous bank accounts, and other such services. Profits are invested to pay for deliveries of cocaine, heroin, and synthetic drugs. As one interviewee emphasized, this is how the new generations of mobsters now line their pockets with nothing more than a computer. The amount of money to be made is enormous. As he concluded, "Cosa Nostra infiltrates and always thrives where there is money."

Case Study: Operation Akhua

Operation Akhua (Italian government's Ministero dell'Interno Report 2, 2020: 54) was carried out by the Carabinieri on February 4, 2020 in the provinces of Rome, Naples, Varese, Reggio Calabria, Cagliari, Oristano, Trento, and also in Spain, culminating in the arrest of 33 individuals belonging to different 'Ndrangheta families who were charged with the trafficking and distribution of narcotic substances as well as providing illegal access to online systems. This case showed how hybrid criminality works methodically, with different roles assigned to each criminal group. One group was involved directly in the illegal trafficking of narcotic substances along the Rome–Cagliari route, headed by two members of the Bellocco 'Ndrangheta clan based in Rosarno. A second group – under the leadership of two brothers belonging to the Camorra's Licciardi clan based in the district of Secondigliano near Naples – was involved with the territorial distribution. A third group coordinated the drug supply channels in South America.

A case such as this shows how hybrid criminality requires a global coordination system among different criminal actors. As Lavorgna and Antonopoulos (2022: 150) put it:

> Despite the heterogeneity of the criminal markets and networks ... some key aspects are increasingly emerging in cybercrime research as pivotal, such as the glocalization of

cybercrimes (that is, the permanent intertwining of the global and local dimensions, which coexist as two sides of the same coin), with its obvious implications in terms of: the need for both international cooperation and the improvement of local capacities; the fluid and transient nature of many relevant networks, with some of the individuals involved lacking a serious commitment towards a specific form of criminality, or towards criminality at all; the need to move beyond rigid and fictional distinctions when we study the relationship between the online and the offline, with the physical and digital dimensions of crimes being different in their manifestations, but also entangled.

Case Study: Apostolos Trovias

In July 2021, a Dark Web vendor called Apostolos Trovias, nicknamed "The Bull," was arrested and charged with securities fraud and money laundering. His case emphasized again how a single operator can become a self-styled cybercriminal. Trovias had engaged in insider trading, attempting to buy and then sell insider information on his website, including trading tips, weekly and monthly plans, and pre-release earnings reports in exchange for bitcoin. He eventually came to the attention of law enforcement when he attempted to sell information – unbeknownst to him – to undercover agents of the Internal Revenue Service and the FBI.

This case shows again how any criminal entity – a single operator, a spontaneous start-up gang, or traditional mafias – can use the Dark Web to buy and sell scammed proprietary information from companies. Trovias's extended and uninterrupted presence on the Dark Web also highlighted how anyone could use it to operate under the radar. As the United Nations Office on Drugs and Crime's report on Dark Net Trafficking (2020) has pointed out, the Dark Web marketplaces showcase how many criminal activities are now established, coordinated, and exchanged by any criminal actor. Cyberspace has empowered anyone to either act independently or be recruited by organized criminal groups. The dark marketplaces now constitute a kind of cybercrime ecosystem where diverse criminal actors come together, including drug cartels, hackers, and the traditional criminal organizations. As the case of Mexico's Zetas and Gulf Cartel illegal scheme showed, this ecosystem has made it possible to adapt traditional criminalities, such as kidnapping, to new objectives. The two gangs were involved in the 2013 kidnapping of telecommunications engineer Felipe Peréz, forcing him to help create cyber networks to assist them in carrying out their illegal activities (Quintero, 2017).

Case Study: Emojis as Criminal Cant

As mentioned, street gangs such as the Crips and the Bloods have adopted emojis as part of a code of gang identity and a means of visual communication, often turning the semantics of emojis on its head. For instance, the two thumbs up emoji does not mean what it usually does – "everything is fine." Instead, it is the symbol of membership to the Harlem Crips. They use the two thumbs-up emoji, with the knuckles facing each other, because it resembles the letter "H" – for "Harlem." As such, emoji use is morphing into a criminal cant among various gangs, where the emoji meaning becomes specialized. A salient example of this can be seen in the use of the moonfish and snowman emojis by drug dealers broadly to sell cocaine via the Internet. As Holgado (2020) points out:

> The use of emojis has become commonplace in communication between members of terrorist or criminal organizations. ... The use of emojis in the criminal context is extremely varied, but there is still a common thread: the signs work like a code that is understandable only to members of the criminal organization.

As law scholar Marilyn McMahon has put it: "Criminals have rushed to adopt these technologies which make it easier for them while complicating that of the police officers who investigate their actions" (cited in Holgado, 2020). The police have realized that they need to decode the emoji cant according to the situation – criminal organizations might commission a killing with weapons emojis or order a credit card scam with emojis such as money bags or credit card ones.

Criminal organizations are constantly revising the meanings of the symbols they use, as well as keeping up to date with changes in the symbolism that technology makes available, allowing them to devise new ways of communicating cryptically and menacingly.

Epilogue

As Misha Glenny (2018) has remarked, the traditional mafias may have migrated to cyberspace and its dark marketplaces, but they have held on to many of their traditions, which they have adapted to the operationality of these marketplaces, at the same time that they have adapted to the world of the matrix psychologically and socially. The newly organized criminality involves the interaction of three dimensions, which can be envisioned as being concentric – Dark Mafia (represented by D in Figure 3.1), which exists at the operational core of hybrid criminality; encircling this is the visible Internet mafia (represented by I), standing for the use of social media and the regular Internet by the criminals in public ways; and encircling the previous two is the real-world mafia (represented by R) which carries out the physical aspects of criminality in geographical spaces.

The Hollywood image of Al-Capone, a mobster who lived by the gun and an archaic moral code, has started to fade from the popular imagination, perhaps because it no longer fits into this concentric model. Beginning in 2011, when the FBI arrested 127 mobsters in New York City, leaving the Colombo and Gambino crime families depleted, the Capone figure started receding to the margins of nostalgia. In March 2017, the FBI continued its crackdown on the Lucchese and Bonanno families, further eroding the lure of the wise guy figure.

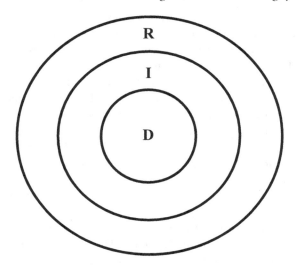

FIGURE 3.1 Mafia 2.0

For many mobsters, the world of the matrix is now a fact of criminal life. They live in two main regions of the matrix, the dark ones where illegal marketplaces emerge, based on alliances among drug cartels, criminal groups, and hackers; while the surface regions are where they put themselves on ostentatious display and from where they now exert a new kind of influence on the modern imagination. In many countries, mobsters are now online influencers and producers of content, with their autobiographies and retrospective accounts becoming known through social media sites and podcasts. Mafia-type organizations have gone from pseudo-historical entities to online avatars where they seem to enjoy the instant celebrity status that cyberspace offers them (Chapter 4).

The Ramnicu Valcea case discussed here constitutes the first true chapter in the story of hybrid criminality. Even though the Romanian group had no previous links to organized crime, nor desired to have them, it was able to establish and conduct a sophisticated criminal operation using basic technical skills. The group also conducted real-world crimes and entered into corruption alliances with politicians and authorities. Ever since, it has become clear that technologies are crucial for the conduct of criminal activities. In the same way that sites like eBay and Amazon have changed how people shop for goods in the legitimate economy, the Dark Web has allowed criminals to run a large part of their illegal economy and to continue operating it even from prison. Joseph Graziano, an associate of the Gambino crime family, who was arrested in 2015, did not stop his illegal gambling operations. While in prison, the operations continued online, coordinated by his intermediaries. He understood that it does not matter what side of the screen one inhabits; either side can be used to enact criminal operations uninterrupted. To understand the power, reach, and allure of the Mafia 2.0 we must clearly look beyond the classic theories, as Lavorgna (2020) has also cogently argued. Crime results from opportunism – and the mafias are nothing if not opportunists of the highest order. Already in 2010, a report on global crime by the United Nations Office on Drugs and Crime emphasized the relationship between the inherent opportunism of criminal organizations and the evolving world of the Internet – a remark that still holds today:

> In the past quarter century, global governance has failed to keep pace with economic globalization. Therefore, as unprecedented openness in trade, finance, travel and communication has created economic growth and well-being, it has also given rise to massive opportunities for criminals to make their business prosper.

4

COOL MAFIA

Prologue

Today, street gangs show off their crimes on social media platforms so as to promote their criminal reputations, using new communicative strategies, such as emojis, to fashion their identity symbolically, and displaying a similar pattern of clothing styles with tattoos, bling jewelry, and close-cut hairstyles. Young mafiosi now upload their promotional selfies to Instagram and TikTok, posing with guns and semiautomatic weapons, conveying an ominous and fearsome criminal image, at the same time that they put on display their glamorous lifestyles on the same social media pages. A mafioso today is a vastly different personage than the traditional one, emblemized by the figure of Al Capone, who was also brutal, at the same time that he was a celebrity figure created by the film industry. He lived by a code of secrecy and honor. In the Internet Age what used to be hidden is now showcased in conceited, self-absorbed ways on the computer screen. The era of social media networks has spawned a new generation of criminals who are increasingly using technology for both professional and vainglorious reasons. Even a quick scan of social media platforms shows how they are being used as a public criminal tool to do the things that were done in secret in the past – to recruit members, intimidate, exploit, and coerce victims. Even quarrels among criminal groups now originate on Facebook, TikTok, or other social media platforms.

DOI: 10.4324/9781003278597-5

Cyberspace is inhabited by three major types of criminals, mirroring their counterparts in real space – the single lone wolf hacker, the spontaneously formed criminal gang, which has no historical connection to crime in the offline world, and the traditional organized crime syndicates that have migrated to cyberspace advantageously as hybrid criminal organizations. There are differences among the three, but the one that unites them psychologically is vainglory. The figure of the "wise guy," long before the advent of the Internet, is evidence that this has always been the chink in the armor of traditional mafias since it brings out the mafioso from the shadows into the social limelight. The wise guy was created by Hollywood as a handsome, slick, and brawny macho man. The migration to cyberspace has brought about a refashioning of this image – the mafioso now sees himself as part of a dualistic personality (as discussed in the previous chapter) – a cloak-and-dagger figure who inhabits the dark regions of cyberspace and a personage addicted to social media, where he presents himself as an ersatz celebrity. Being in sync with the times, the wise guy is now a "cool guy," bragging about his flashy lifestyle and sending out threats to victims for all to see.

Initially, mafia-type organizations kept away from the public limelight, portraying themselves as humble and honorable societies, allowing their exploits and mythologies to be told through legends, tales, and other oral narratives. When new gangsters emerged in America, starting in the 1920s, during the Prohibition era, the first break away from this portrayal occurred, with bootleggers dressing with sartorial elegance as they frequented the clubs to which they provided illegal alcohol. Hollywood instantly realized that this new public criminal figure had great appeal and could thus be exploited for entertainment. The humble-looking gangster thus became transformed into a celebrity on the movie screen. As the matrix came into the world, the Mafia's Hollywood-shaped wise guy morphed into a cool guy on the computer screen. The traditional mafias portrayed themselves as chivalric knights to fit in with the beliefs that resonated with earlier cultures, which allowed them to present themselves as protectors of the rustic classes – hence the term *Cavalleria Rusticana* (rustic chivalry) used commonly to describe this historical phase of the Italian mafias. The move from the chivalric phase to the wise guy one started in the Prohibition era, symbolized (as mentioned) by Al Capone. He was one of the first mobsters to portray himself as a modern movie-style celebrity rather than as a brave and humble rustic knight. Today, it is not the Hollywood screen that spreads the images of mafiosi, but social media memes and viral videos often circulated at first by the mafiosi themselves.

As Richard Dawkins (1976) — the originator of the term *meme* long before the Internet — claimed, memes are psychologically effective because they embed themselves in people's minds. In some ways, memes and memetic culture are a retrieval of ancient mythic culture, which was episodic and based on narrative fragments that people amalgamated into legends and sagas passed on by word of mouth. Memes are the new fragments, assigning a new type of mythic stature to criminals that are in sync with contemporary digital forms of representation. This might itself have countervailing effects on the traditions of the mafias, since it might deconstruct their constitution, as will be discussed in the next chapter. Suffice it to say that memetic culture is hardly an organic historical culture, requiring a central narrative, told and retold in various forms. The narrative unity of the mafia's self-sustaining myths of origin is thus at risk of dissipation in the world of memes. Memetic culture is fragmented, self-referential, and highly intertextual; it is not cohesive and linear, going from a historical point in time to another subsequent one. So the question becomes: Will mafia culture, as previously understood, change drastically due to the rise of memetic culture? This chapter will look at how memetic culture and the social media world, more generally, are refashioning the image of mafiosi and altering the historical flow of mafia culture itself.

The Wise Guy

The term "wise guy," used to describe members of the American Cosa Nostra, came into public use in the 1970s, primarily through the movies of that era. It corresponds more or less to the Italian word *furbo* ("clever person"), denoting a male person who knows how to comport himself in public as a tough, no-nonsense, personage and who is highly attractive because of his slick appearance and "bad boy" character. There was no such figure in the original mafias, who expected their members to be *uomini d'onore* ("men of honor"). The central tenet of the original honor code demanded that a mafioso must defend the honor of his crime family — this is why the Calabrian mafia refers to itself as the *Onorata Società* (the "Honored Society").

Although not named a wise guy, the appearance of this figure (as mentioned) is traceable to Al Capone, who gained notoriety during the Prohibition era as a bootlegger and boss of the Chicago Outfit gang. Capone was born in New York City to Italian immigrant parents, joining a local gang as a teenager and taking a job as a bouncer in brothels run by mobsters. He moved to Chicago and became a bodyguard for a criminal organization that illegally supplied alcohol. When Capone became a bootlegger himself, he carried out his criminal business not only with violent means but also by corrupting police officers and government officials, which allowed him free rein as a *capo* operating openly in public. Capone was attracted to the limelight; as a result, he forged a new identity for mobsters in America, radically different from the honored man image of the past. He dressed up in an elegant suit and tie, fedora hat, shiny black shoes, and smoked a cigar constantly, becoming the standard "look" of the wise guy in movies and real life. Capone further ensconced this image into the public eye by making donations to various charities, being called a "modern-day Robin Hood" by the media at the time. However, the Saint Valentine's Day Massacre, in which seven gang rivals were murdered on the morning of February 14, 1929, by the Chicago Outfit, led by Capone, damaged his image, leading the media to dub him instead as "Public Enemy Number One."

As Klaus von Lampe (2016: 23) has remarked, during Prohibition "organized crime no longer referred to an amorphous 'criminal class' but to 'gangsters and racketeers' who were organized in 'gangs,' 'syndicates,' and 'criminal organizations,' following 'big master criminals' who functioned as 'powerful leaders of organized crime.'" It was then that the conditions were ripe for a new image to emerge – the image created by Al Capone. Capone became as famous as any movie star of the era, catching the attention of Hollywood, which enshrined the wise guy image of a well-dressed, attractive but ruthless macho man mobster into the modern-day history of cinema and criminology. One of the most famous gangster movies of all time, *Little Caesar* (1931), was modeled on the wise guy persona. The leading actor, Edward G. Robinson, attended Capone's trial in 1931 for tax evasion to take a close-up look at Capone for crafting his character role. The movie embedded the image of the American wise guy mafioso as a real, recognizable character, once and for all. The film's protagonist, Cesare "Rico" Bandello was a ruthless mobster with street savvy and gritty toughness but who also lived by the code of honor that his gang imposed on him. Hollywood and Cosa Nostra had become perfect partners in crime (so to speak). The former created the wise guy figure, fashioning him after real-life mobsters such as Al Capone, and the latter imitated the Hollywood model in real life. The success of *Little Caesar* made it clear that popular and criminal culture had formed a dynamic partnership, reinforced a year later, in 1932, with the film *Scarface*, which was based on Capone's life. Decades later, the Hollywood-manufactured wise guy image was further embedded with the iconic movie, *The Godfather* (1972), in which the main character, Don Vito Corleone, was seen often as well-dressed, and his demeanor demure, measured, and composed, yet defiant. Don Vito's "look, talk, and walk" stereotypically reflected Hollywood's idea of what a wise guy was all about. That image spilled over into mafioso culture itself, which ensconced it further as a lifestyle model.

As the Internet came into existence, and as criminal gangs migrated to cyberspace to carry out their operations, the Al Capone-Don Vito figure of the wise guy, imitated by countless mafiosi, started to dissipate from both the screen and real criminal life, remaining mainly a nostalgic image, revisited by movies and documentaries. The image is seen as a ludicrous one among the new generations of mafiosi, who have carved out a new look for themselves on the computer screen. In his new criminal disguise, the mafioso carries out his activities in the shadows of the Dark Web, avoiding the reach of the authorities; while in his public disguise, he shows off his tattooed body, his lavish lifestyle, and his "cool" tough guy persona to the social media generation. Nowadays, the mafiosi have left behind the Al Capone "dapper don" figure, replacing it with the flashy "cool guy" online character, who brags openly about his criminal exploits. The break from mafia traditions could not be greater. If the rules of the past were in force, the young mafiosi would be threatened with death for acting ostentatiously in public and exposing themselves to police observation through their reckless posts. For investigators, the mafioso's social media vainglory has made it possible to extract a treasure trove of information from the posts; and for criminologists many insights into the mind of contemporary mafiosi can be attained, given that they now record their thoughts, feelings, and aspirations on their posts, which often spread virally.

The Cool Guy

A paradox of the Mafia 2.0 is that its hybrid operationality, with all the changes that it has brought about to the traditional structure of criminal organizations, has still not led to the complete elimination of the ancient codes – the large outer concentric circle in the model of mafia-type organizations discussed in this book (Chapter 3). Their initiation rites continue as in the past but perhaps with less value among younger generation. Traditional organized crime has gone from a rural mafia, based on a rustic code of criminal honor, to an industrialized one, as evidenced by the Cosa Nostra syndicates of the twentieth century and their wise guy constituency, to the Internet one participating fully in the current information society. This three-phase evolution is shown diagrammatically in Figure 4.1.

Even without sophisticated or expensive digital technologies, mobsters can now carry out summits among themselves, organize criminal activities, and carry out new kinds of joint operations, through the computer screen. The networking capacities introduced by the Internet have made it possible for different criminal parties to gain and strengthen consensus, which is essential for the survival of individual organizations. And as mafia-type organizations turn more and more to social media networks, they are creating a new brand image among younger generations, so to attract them to the new world of hybrid criminality. The wise guy has moved to the other side of the matrix, where he is recasting himself as a dualistic character – a combination of the dark operator on the Dark Web and a fashionable social media personality on the surface web. The case of Vincenzo Torcasio, a boss of the 'Ndrangheta, was one of the first ones exemplifying how this dualistic persona has come into existence (Chapter 2). Recall that Torcasio had constructed a Facebook page, called *Onore e dignità*, "Honour and Dignity," which he used to promote his cool guy image, while using it to issue threats, before the page was shut down upon his

FIGURE 4.1 The Main Phases of Mafia Evolution

incarceration in 2017. The heading of "honour" and "dignity" was a clear allusion to the original mafia code, while the profile's content was anything but a portrayal of dignity or honor.

Torcasio's page consisted of an eclectic admixture of images, quotes from famous writers, wise sayings, and pictures of large sums of money. Many of his posts decried the fate of imprisoned mafiosi: Chiedo e pretendo processi giusti. *Non indiziari e no libero convincimento dei giudici!* ("I ask and demand fair trials. No circumstantial and no free convictions of the judges"), *Chiedo rispetto per i diritti dei carcerati!* ("I ask for respect for the rights of all prisoners"), *La dignità per ogni detenuto* ("Dignity for every prisoner"), *E sono contro la tortura del 41 Bis!* ("And I am against the torture of 41-bis"), etc. The latter message refers to a provision that allows the Minister of Justice to suspend ordinary regimes for prisoners and keep them in isolation. With over 18,000 followers, Torcasio had become a social media celebrity, showing to what extent mafias bosses had moved away from maintaining a low public profile to avoid attention from law enforcement towards embracing the social media spotlight. New York City mobster John Gotti had also courted publicity and media attention in the 1980s. But he could hardly gain the broad international attention that the social media universe offers today. Moreover, once apprehended by police, the wise guy of the past would disappear from the public eye. In the social media era, this is hardly the case. For instance, Torcasio's Facebook page remains online, even after his arrest in 2017, with new posts focusing on the dangers betrayal by those who turned State witnesses and on paying respect to famous Italian organized crime bosses from the past. Torcasio continued to live on in cyberspace, as he served his prison sentence.

As this case indicates, the new generation of mafiosi has embraced digital culture. Videos of young mobsters posing with automatic weapons, displaying flashy jewelry, and singing rap songs are found throughout social media platforms. Ironically, the barrage of new posts has marginalized mobsters such as Torcasio, who, in a matter of a few years, were seen as old-fashioned to the subsequent online-based criminals. Torcasio saw this as a travesty, writing on his page: "If the past comes back to find you try and avoid it. There is no room for those who have turned their backs on you." But his advice went unheeded, as the younger generations organized criminals on social media have seemingly forgotten (or ignored) past achievements of mafia figures, aiming merely to attract large numbers of followers as fans, as they carve out their cool guy image almost daily, glamorizing their crimes as part of an ever-morphing macho lifestyle. They are also using the Internet to carry out a war of words, as exemplified by a case when the Di Lauro clan in Naples labeled the rival Amato-Pagano clan as "the secessionists." The latter responded by rebranding itself as *gli spagnoli* ("the Spaniards"), a nickname recalling clan leader Raffaele Amato's time as a fugitive in the Spanish Costa del Sol, and thus conveying criminal bravado.

A search of social media platforms has made it clear that such images spread broadly throughout the world of organized crime, presenting an attractive alternative lifestyle to many young people. Aware of the pull of social media, many criminal organizations now simply allow the younger generations to literally do whatever they want online, in stark contrast to the strict controls that were once exacted by leaders over the conduct of their young recruits. For example, the social media posts by the sons of Joaquín Guzman Loera (El Chapo), published after his arrest in 2016, illustrate this "anything goes" behavior, amplifying the lifestyle patterns of their cartel predecessors, designed to flaunt their wealth and macho attractiveness, with images of luxurious parties, attractive women, exotic animals, piles of cash, and big guns. Similarly, the younger members of the Italian mafias boast of their luxurious lifestyles on social networks; in Japan, the Yakuza have even created a webpage to appeal directly to the new generations. Thanks to the Internet, such sites can be accessed from any place on the globe, spreading the glare of criminal lifestyles worldwide. Social media networks have clearly replaced Hollywood and television; through them the figure of the cool guy surfaces broadly, attracting recruits. The same platforms are also now where authorities can monitor organized crime groups' messages. The arrest of the Camorra fugitive Michele Di Nardo was the result of certain statements posted by his girlfriend on Facebook, as she responded to his threatening statements towards her. Gone are the days when mobsters hissed threats over the phone, or sent *pizzini*.

Today, bosses cannot resist the urge to post photos and messages on social media, no matter the consequences. In 2011, a fugitive boss of the Camorra, Salvatore D'Avino, was arrested, after his Moroccan girlfriend had heedlessly posted two photos of herself and D'Avino on the Marbella beach of the Costa del Sol, in Spain, alerting the authorities as to his location. Similarly, another fugitive, Roberto Di Girolamo, a member of the Stidda, a rival clan of Cosa Nostra based in Gela, Sicily, published images of himself and his family hiding in Switzerland, allowing the police to find him a few days later. Donato Fratto, who was wanted for his alleged association with the 'Ndrangheta and who had a passion for motorcycles, posted on Facebook that he would be participating in a gathering of motorbike enthusiasts in Sardinia, leading the Carabinieri to arrest him there. Palermo mobster Salvino Bonomolo, who used Facebook as a work tool, under a false name, so that he could exchange private messages with his accomplices in Italy and Latin America, boasted about a drug trafficking operation on his page, which allowed the authorities to track him down in Venezuela.

Such cases raise the question of why members of organized crime so willingly expose themselves online. An obvious and trivial reason is to carry out communications between members in a rapid way, as Maurizio De Lucia, the chief prosecutor of Palermo, has affirmed after examining the social media posts of members of the local mafias. But another reason is, in our view, that social networks allow the new generation of mobsters to carve out a cool guy image for themselves that is in step with the times. As the Michele Di Nardo case emphasized, mobsters today have no qualms about showing themselves in a tanned photo alongside their girlfriends, despite being sought by the police. The luxurious cars, bottles of champagne, lavish resort places, and beautiful girls on mobsters' social media pages reinforce the cool guy image – even if they constitute clues as to their location or intentions. Wealth, machismo, and power have always been intrinsic to the lure of criminal lifestyle. To paraphrase statements made by one of our interviewed police officers, the social media pages that mafiosi create have an underlying motivation – beyond communication with members – to increase their popularity and to gain social acceptance through likes and shares.

Vainglory

To reiterate, current mobsters' primary motivation for using social media is actually an age-old one – vainglory – which has been the mafias' Achilles heel even in the past. Elegant suits, hats, slicked down hair, shiny shoes, and cigars became part of a wise guy gangster look in the era of Prohibition, to the point that some mobsters would never be caught in public without the appropriate dress code. An anecdote told about Frank Costello, a crime boss of the Luciano family (now

FIGURE 4.2   Frank Costello, American Mobster, Testifying Before the Kefauver Committee Investigating Organized Crime

Source: No copyright restriction known. Staff photographer reproduction rights transferred to Library of Congress through Instrument of Gift.

Genovese), brings this out perfectly. As Reynolds (2006: 189) notes, Costello "was the original dapper don, sporting thousand-dollar tailored suits, custom-made shoes, perfect manicures and a bullet-proof haircut." His lawyer even warned Costello to dress unpretentiously in a court appearance because it might negatively influence the perceptions of middle-class jury members (Figure 4.2). Costello purportedly responded: "I'd rather lose the goddamn case" (Reynolds, 2006: 190).

The Costello image is imprinted nostalgically in the popular imagination, thanks to the movies and television. But among the younger mafiosi today, it is seen as a remnant of a previous time at best and as a ludicrous caricature at worst. Mafia men today dress in various styles, from designer clothes to hoodies and T-shirts, depending on age or clan. Along with hyperbolic forms of bragging on media sites, it is clear that the behavioral codes of the past have gone by the wayside in cyberspace, rendering the criminal clans throughout the world indistinguishable in their appearance, behavior, and language. A camorrista is now no different in appearance than any other mobster, no matter what country he comes from. The days of Costello-type style, which were meant to differentiate the macho wise guy from everyone else, have literally dissipated in cyberspace, where a new cool guy code has become the norm, spreading uniformly throughout the globe, leveling off the appearance and behavior of different clans into one generic one. Members of all criminal stripes now memorialize themselves with the same cool guy code, with little variation, via social media. Our search of pages managed by the new generation of mobsters in Italy has indicated that there is, in fact, little difference between the physical look and dress of a camorrista or an 'Ndranghetista – all seem to aspire to conform to the same appearance code. A social media post we found by Domenico Bellocco constitutes a case in point. Bellocco is the grandson of an 'Ndrangheta boss. Unlike the modest and unassuming portrait of his grandfather, who always dressed in a suit and tie in public, Bellocco wears T-shirts, jeans, and other items that make up the cool guy look. He also presents himself as a rap artist.

The difference between Bellocco's appearance and that of Costello is striking – there is nothing in common. The only thing that they share is vainglory – expressed in different ways. Significantly, Bellocco's rap videos went viral. Released under a stage name, Glock 21, they feature fast cars, heavy weapons, and large bling jewelry, with profane and even obscene lyrics that convey an insouciant attitude devoid of modesty or a sense of shame. Bellocco has consistently denied that he is involved in crime and that the videos were made simply for art's sake. Interestingly, one of his videos, called *Chiamami Boss* ("Call Me Boss"), showed Bellocco rapping on the hood of a Lamborghini car as a blonde woman danced salaciously in front of him. This image shatters all previous wise guy images, catapulting the cool guy into a world of cultural pastiche and cultural indefiniteness, where he blends in indistinctly with the image of any online celebrity or musician.

As the older clan leaders start to disappear, those taking their place have started to cut ties with the past, not only in terms of organizational structure but also in the area of lifestyles and appearance. Moreover, social media have led to the proliferation of random cliques of adolescents who meet on TikTok and then go to the streets to cause trouble, gaining attention for their egregious acts of violence often to audition for clan membership – an absolute taboo in traditional mafia culture, where initiation rites were kept highly secret and ritualized. The Italian Anti-Mafia Investigation Directorate's 2019 report (Direzione Investigativa Antimafia, 2019) labeled these online videos as a "Camorra academy," where aspiring mobsters post their street gang activities on social media to show their mettle to the real Camorra. The report also highlighted that street gangs, called colloquially in Italy, "baby gangs," act with the same level of violence as the real gangs. Their posts show them bragging about their weapons, tattoos, motorbikes, and love of "traplodic" – a fusion of "trap" (a rap genre) and neomelodic music associated with the Camorra. In several posts we visited online, we also noted the frequent use of symbols to reinforce allegiance to Camorra, including lion emojis – a sign of strength and aggression – to communicate to the real camorristi that they were ready for duty. We also found that the eyes emoji symbolized loyalty, since it represents the Neapolitan saying, "He who knows the game will stay quiet." The use of street slang was also a common strategy. In one TikTok posting, a street thug just released from prison was described as "our ruler of the *piazza*" – slang for a spot where people deal drugs.

The posts display what the new criminal cool guy is all about. While the rise of baby gangs may be tied to various sociological and cultural factors, the point here is that they literally design themselves with the same cool guy look of the real mafiosi – showing their faces to the world via the screen and thus breaking away from any code of secrecy of the past. As Marcello Ravveduto (2018: 57) has written, the traditional organized crime, like the Camorra, appear in "various stages of virtual rooting." And this has profoundly altered their public image. To see a junior mafioso today dressed in a style that recalls the dapper don era would be not only out of step with the times but also perceived as ridiculous. Mobsters are a reflection of society. And times change for everyone.

However, as in the past, vainglory exposes mobsters to criminal investigators. Significant in this area was the rise of TikTok in 2021, which became a favorite platform of the gangs. An example comes from Bolivia in 2021, where a narco-gang had uploaded videos to its TikTok accounts, showing them participating in the manufacturing of cocaine. They also posted videos and selfies of themselves in a boat loaded with drugs and bragging about the luxury muscle vehicles they could purchase, thanks to the drug trade (reported in Carrillo, 2022). Gang members had thousands of followers and even foolishly shared their location in the comments sections. As a result, investigators were able to locate and arrest two of the young men on drug trafficking charges in Cochabamba. Interestingly, others posted messages about the arrest on TikTok, portraying the detained individuals as fearless warriors.

Like the Italian baby gangs, narco-gangs in Mexico are now flooding social media platforms, posting pictures of weapons and lavish wealth. We found, interestingly, that there is a large group of narco-juniors who claim to be related to, or associated with, the former head of the Sinaloa Cartel, El Chapo and his children, calling itself *La* Chapiza gang, to indicate loyalty to El Chapo's children (see also Carrillo, 2022). In one video, an armed, masked police officer is seen asking a member to lower the window of his car. The gangster mocks the officer saying, "We are La Chapiza." The officer immediately raises his hand and says: "All's good, thank you, everything's in order," and walks away. The individuals in the video looked exactly like their counterparts in the Italian baby gangs, with the same attire and bodily postures, indicating toughness and nonchalance at once. The video also foolishly (perhaps indifferently) provided information as to the location of the actual gang members. Overall, the new generations of criminals and mobsters are everyday participants in the world of the matrix, entering it enthusiastically, incapable of staying away from the screen. As neuroscience research has been showing (He et al., 2017), maybe the reason for all this is that social media are addictive, producing dopamine, the so-called chemical of pleasure. The neuroscientists found that dopamine releases occur when likes and comments are posted on social media platforms, prompting the same neural chemistry triggered by addictive recreational drugs. The constant stream of likes, emojis, and shares causes the brain's reward area to activate the same kind of chemical reaction triggered by drugs like cocaine (Lembke, 2021). This type of research is, in a word, suggestive of why young criminals use social media constantly, often to their detriment.

One of the most famous cases showing how mafiosi will risk exposure and capture, just to connect with others via social media, goes back to the 2010 arrest of one of Italy's most-wanted mafia bosses, who had been a fugitive for months, namely Pasquale Manfredi, a vicious 'Ndrangheta boss, arrested after being tracked down through his Facebook account. Detectives were able to locate his hideout using electronic tracking equipment (reported in Wise, 2010). Manfredi had used the pseudonym "Scarface," which he adopted after seeing the 1983 movie. He logged on to his Facebook account so often that the police were able to identify his Internet address and thus find his hideout, in the town of Isola Capo Rizzuto, in the province of Crotone in Calabria, where he lived alone in a basement apartment. The hideout, which was tiny, still managed to fit two computers and a treadmill and weight bar for keeping in shape. Like many other mobsters, Manfredi got caught because he had a Facebook addiction. Ironically, Manfredi was an admirer of the Cuban wise guy, Tony Montana. But unlike the wise guy character, Manfredi had transformed himself into a cool guy mafioso who could not stay away from his addictive drug – Facebook.

Case Studies: IV

Bosses who use social media are replacing the bosses of the past, showing an addictive need to show themselves off publicly. Sicilian boss Domenico Palazzotto, for instance, craved to show himself on his yachts or in his limousine while drinking champagne, as we found on many of his posts. The Sicilian Mafia, known for its clandestine traditions and rituals, has clearly moved on from the days of *omertà* to those of the matrix, where reality and hyperreality are no longer differentiated psychologically. As our police sources confirmed, the new bosses use social media pages every day not solely to communicate with each other but more significantly to show off their power and wealth. As Marcello Ravveduto explained, the Camorra's use of TikTok to spread its messages makes sense for both practical and ostentatious reasons: "Criminal organizations and social media have one thing in common, a network," and thus, as the "Camorra's visibility on TikTok grows, so too does its recruiting pool and its brand image."

The case studies discussed here are intended as portraits of the cool guy, reflecting a radical transition from the wise guy persona. Today, mafia identity is literally performed on social media platforms, indicating that it is no longer perceived in the traditional ways.

Case Study: Facebook

A 2016 Facebook post by Salvatore Riina, Jr., son of the infamous mobster, convicted of assassinating anti-mafia prosecutors Giovanni Falcone and Paolo Borsellino in 1992, is a case in point of how present-day mafiosi use social media for reasons of vainglory, self-promotion, and to brag about past exploits and associations. The post is a self-made promotional one where Riina, Jr. announces the publication of his autobiographical book, *Riina: Family Life*, with self-proclamations about the importance of the book, which he purportedly wrote to set the record straight about his family, portraying his father as a caring and loving man in contrast with the facts, given that Riina senior was one of the bloodiest and most heartless bosses of Mafia history.

The post garnered over 700 likes and 1,100 comments. Scrolling through the comments, however, it becomes clear that Riina had exposed himself to the kind of critique that mafiosi of the past would have absolutely wanted to avoid. In addition to a large number of positive comments, there were also a significant number of critiques and attacks on both the post and the book itself, such as the following [translation ours]: "The people who order this book suck"; "Why haven't you written about all the innocent souls that that [expletive] of your father slaughtered?"; "Don't you ever think that he [your father] caressed you with hands dirty with blood?" "I feel like vomiting to read the comments of mafiosi and admirers of mafiosi." But Riina, Jr. conveniently ignored the negative comments, subsequently posting a renewed invitation to purchase his book [translation ours]: "Thanks to all who have given me their affection and support . . . and to those who stay awake at night to post negative comments . . . writing bad things that do not apply to me."

Riina, Jr.'s use of Facebook to promote himself and his father as modern-day heroes, attracting broad public attention, even if it is ephemeral, shows how the current-day mobster cool guy thinks. Posts by other mobsters reveal a similar display of vainglory – a compulsive need to become celebrities in the eyes of the world. Long before the Internet Age, pop artist Andy Warhol commented that in an era of celebrities, people feel the unconscious need to gain "fifteen minutes of fame." With the rise of the Internet, Warhol's dictum has proven to be prophetic. Going online like Riina, Jr. would have been unthinkable for the old guard; with some exceptions, it would have been seen as shameful boasting. But in the era of the Mafia 2.0, the search for those 15 minutes of fame supersedes any previous code of honor.

Another case in point is that of already mentioned Domenico Palazzotto, a member of Cosa Nostra – a cool guy who put himself on display on Facebook daily to show off his body and luxuriant lifestyle, with photos of himself lounging as he drinks champagne. Palazzotto was the head of the clan of the Arenella district of Palermo – a major player in the drug trafficking trade. Like Riina, Jr., he wanted to establish a link between himself and important figures in Mafia history. In one of his 2014 posts he made the following statement [translation ours]: "My father's uncle was Paolo Palazzotto, who murdered the famous American Italian policeman Joe Petrosino, on behalf of [Don Vito] Cascio Ferro." The murder of Petrosino goes back to 1909, constituting an unsolved case. Although Palazzotto started suspecting that he was being intercepted, he could not stay away from Facebook, continuing to brag about his historically significant Mafia family ties, and excoriating the persecution from authorities to which someone like himself is subjected [translation ours]: "Blessed are those who will be persecuted by justice, because theirs is the kingdom of heaven" (paraphrasing the Gospel according to Matthew).

A perusal of Palazzotto's Facebook pages reveals an arrogant attitude that extends even to the recruits he was trying to attract to his clan. In one post, he jokes superciliously with a wannabe mafioso, who had asked him about joining his clan [translation ours]: "Do I need to send a CV?"; to which Palazzotto replies: "Yes, brother. We need to look over your criminal record. We do not take on people with clean backgrounds. Join my team. We are the strongest, ha ha ha."

Operation Apocalypse arrested Palazzotto in 2014, one of the largest takedowns of Cosa Nostra by the Italian state. At one point, he was overheard by the authorities in an intercepted phone conversation bragging to a fellow mobster that his uncle was Paolo Palazzotto, Petrosino's killer, as he had claimed on his Facebook post. The Petrosino murder had been investigated in the United States and in Italy since 1909. Despite the unwitting proxy divulgence by Palazzotto, the case has not been reopened to find Petrosino's killer.

Case Study: TikTok

In 2020, a video was uploaded to TikTok, shot inside a prison, which provided a prototypical portrait of cool guy mobsters today, who are constantly keeping up to date with trends in social media technologies and selected musical trends. The prison where the video was made was the high-security wing of the Avellino prison, 50 kilometers east of Naples – a prison that houses many camorristi. It featured a song in the neomelodic style. The unidentified inmate's post went viral, again breaking the code of secrecy of the past, as well as showing the extent to which the young mobsters are different in appearance and lifestyle from the ones of the past. It is one of countless examples of young camorristi using TikTok to broadcast their criminal lifestyle and to make themselves known to the higher-ups in the Camorra world (Nocera and D'Avino, 2020). Camorra's TikTok presence offers investigators and criminologists insights into the cultural changes that organized crime is undergoing in the age of social media. Paradoxically, this new world criminal order offers many more career opportunities for women, who appear on social media as brutal criminals themselves, keeping up with their male counterparts, increasingly assuming leading roles in clan hierarchies.

The prison video also highlighted the important role of the *neomelodica* music business in current Camorra culture – a business controlled by both the real and shadow economies in Naples. This musical genre, with its overt melodic references to the traditional *canzone napoletana* style, conveys an undercurrent of ethnic pride in Neapolitan society generally. The music sponsor might be the Camorra, but many claim that it is representing their true sentiments as Neapolitans. In a city where unemployment is chronic, the neomelodic music industry has become, paradoxically, a staple of the Neapolitan economy.

TikTok has become a favorite platform for the Camorra, both as a digital stage for the young mafiosi to show off their criminal qualities and as a recruitment locus, as Marcello Ravveduto discussed with us in an interview: "As the Camorra's visibility on TikTok grows, so too does its recruiting pool, given the allure it has for young people." On any TikTok page, one can see a camorrista showing off his tattoos, singing neomelodica music, and documenting his activities on the streets via videos and selfies – many of which are nothing more than promotional videos. But the use of social media is a double-edged sword since they are valuable sources of information for investigators. In a police operation in April 2021, the Italian authorities found that the conflicts between the Rinaldi and Aprea clans of the eastern area of Naples were fought as much on social media as they were on real ground. They were able to locate a leader of one of the clans, who was under house arrest, because of a TikTok video he posted of himself in a procession driving a Ferrari while visiting his son's communion. The subtext of such a brazen post can be articulated as follows: I am powerful and wealthy, and I am afraid of no one, including the police. In the not-too-distant past, getting attention meant getting on the news and being featured in movies or documentaries. Today, all the mafioso needs to do is upload photos and videos about himself on some social network.

As Nocera and D'Avino (2020) have aptly remarked:

> The Camorra's TikTok presence offers a window into the bigger changes to the structure of the mafia. To be clear, the Camorra doesn't have a members list and there is no absolute way of proving these young TikTok-ers are card-carrying members. This is partly because in the past, being a Camorrista was something of a birthright, with new recruits coming from a few main families. But today, aspiring young mafiosi quickly gain fear and respect with displays of violence on the streets. These younger gangs also post about weapons and the spoils of the criminal lifestyle on social media, ditching the traditional mafia tendency to avoid the limelight.

The TikTok posts we reviewed are also replete with new forms of symbolism, including emojis of lions, guns, and hands joined together to signify brotherhood. In some of them we found fragmented stories of criminal accomplishments, showing little or no regard for the codes of honor of the past. In effect, the cool guy, who lives on social media, has developed his own symbols and narratives. He is a self-styled mafioso with little or no connection to the history of his clan.

Case Study: Emanuele Sibillo

The 2015 ambush killing of nineteen-year-old Emanuele Sibillo, who was the leader of the Sibillo clan, by a rival clan member, brings out the fact that mobster heroes today are no longer lauded in myths and legends that connect them to the historical past but on social media, where they are exalted in memes, emojis, and viral video presentations (Nocera, 2021). The Sibillo clan had been asserting control over several districts in Naples since around 2011, dealing drugs, engaging in racketeering, extorting money from shop owners, and punishing those who were not compliant. The group was eventually brought down in April 2021, when Italian police arrested 21 members of the clan, which continued its operations after Sibillo's death, in homage to his memory, transforming him into a saint-like personage on social media, with tributes coming from both the criminals and the general public alike.

Sibillo had become a model mobster to the online generation, via his signature social media look – soccer haircut, long beard, and dark framed glasses. His rise to fame started in 2011, when at 15 years of age, he was arrested for illegally possessing a firearm. He was sent to a juvenile detention center, where he developed a passion for video recordings. After being released in 2012, he started recruiting juveniles to establish his own clan, rebelling against the old Camorra clans and aiming to take over the city of Naples from them by engaging in aggressive drug dealing and public displays of violence documenting his clan's *stese* (Neapolitan slang for random shootouts on scooters) on posted videos. As Ravveduto explained, Sibillo's online appearance itself "inspired awe and incited violence." Between 2013 and 2015, he adopted a tag, ES17, with ES standing for his initials and 17 for "S," the seventeenth letter of the Italian alphabet. This symbol was splattered on the walls of Naples, as a kind of flag to claim the territory as Sibillo's own. Interestingly, Sibillo was reported to have been a keen fan of the television series, *Gomorrah*, which became the topic of a heated debate in Italy for some time, even accused by a former mayor of Naples as "corroding the brains, souls and hearts of hundreds of very young people" (cited in Nocera, 2021). Sibillo himself was, apparently, the inspiration for the character of "Sangue Blu" ("Blue blood"), who made his appearance in the third season of the series.

The Sibillo case reveals that a single young criminal had the ability to rise to fame on his own because of social media, which he used as a powerful manipulative propaganda tool, boasting of the lavish lifestyle that crime afforded to someone like himself, posting pictures of expensive clothes, cars, and exclusive restaurants. He became a larger-than-life *scugnizzo* (clever and cunning street boy in Neapolitan slang), who was able to recruit a network of young people to do his bidding. Eventually, an internecine war of rival gangs broke out in Naples in 2015, resulting in more than 40 deaths, including the death of Sibillo. As Nocera (2021) perceptively remarks: "Until his death, Sibillo was at the forefront of a paradigm shift in the Camorra, whose structure now more closely resembles that of South American gangs, rather than the traditional family-based Italian one." As Ravveduto added, the life of such ad hoc gangs, which emerge on social media, provide a *sui generis* sense of ethnic pride: "They use the Neapolitan dialect as their language, to affirm their shared identity." Sibillo's fame was actually memorialized with a bust on an altar in the city right after his death, in front of which young camorristi kneeled, bringing out the degree to which cyberspace now creates its own pseudo-heroes. The Carabinieri finally removed the altar in April 2021 upon the arrest of the clan members.

Case Study: The Hells Angels

The Hells Angels, an outlaw bike gang, aims to present a positive public image of themselves by participating in good deeds for a community, such as local Toy Runs, where members show up with gifts and monetary donations. Like other criminal gangs, the Hells Angels have established a social media presence that has attracted innumerable followers. In 2018, the leader of the Manitoba Nomads, a chapter of the gang, was informed that some of his members had been turned away from a hotel in Winnipeg for wearing their trademark logos. Rather than go to the hotel and use physical intimidation as retaliation, he went on his social media account, imploring his followers to boycott or at least complain about the business (reported in Barghout, 2018).

Supporters took his cue and resorted to Facebook in droves to express their displeasure with the hotel. When the small hotel removed its Facebook page, the bikers and their social media friends turned their ire against the restaurant in the hotel. Within one day, hundreds posted one-star reviews on the restaurant's Facebook page, so as to sully its reputation. The Hells Angels used a new weapon that did not require guns or fists – Facebook – which allowed them and their followers to band together to attack businesses in a new way. They went on their accounts, posting photos of themselves as victorious and showing off their toughness. But even before attacking the hotel and eatery, the same gang had targeted a sports shop, which was supposed to be the starting point for the usual motorcycle ride held in June, using the same technique. The Manitoba Women's Motorcycle Council had organized the event to raise money. In a social media post about the event, organizers stated that the gang's symbolic colors were not welcome. In reaction, the chapter leader implored his Facebook followers to give the store one-star reviews. This got the Council to reverse its decision, allowing the colors. As a result, the leader asked his followers on social media to change their rating to five stars.

In effect, the Hells Angels had discovered that social media could be weaponized. As this case emphasized, gangs and criminal organizations are turning to social media networking sites as ways to intimidate victims. On the other side, such sites have become useful intelligence resources for law enforcement, as mentioned several times, monitoring the gangs to detect wrongdoings and assess their power and reach socially and culturally.

Epilogue

After the infamous Cosa Nostra hitman of the Gambino crime family in New York City, Salvatore ("Sammy the Bull") Gravano, was released from prison in 2017, he instantly took to social media, becoming a daily user of Facebook, Instagram, and YouTube, starting a podcast as well. Gravano was the original wise guy. The fact that he became a cool guy right after his release speaks volumes about how mafia-type organizations are evolving in the world of the matrix, breaking away from every previous canon of *omertà* to which a veteran criminal like Gravano had once pledged his allegiance. The Hollywood godfather kiss of the past has turned into a "like" on social media.

While the ultimate goal of the wise guy and the cool guy is the same – to flaunt strength and power – the reach of the cool guy via social media has rendered all previous forms of criminal celebrity-making obsolete. The social profiles of camorristi, 'ndranghetisti, mafiosi, and many others are followed by thousands of "friends" as their posts generate huge fan bases. The cool guy can show himself as invincible with videos, weaponry, and intimidating captions. Many of them might become bosses not by acclamation of fellow members who evaluate their criminal accomplishments as they move up the hierarchy, but by the number of followers or likes. An example of this trend is the case of Sicilian Mafioso Matteo Messina Denaro, who attracted many followers through his posts, characterized as a new "godfather" and even "savior of the people," catapulting him to the top of Mafia celebrity status via the links. The message is that the cool guy can do whatever he likes, flaunting his appearance, music prefer-ences, and lifestyle to the globe, wiping out anyone who stands in his way, or even shows the slightest amount of disrespect. The cool guy image is all about strutting, insulting, and threatening.

This scenario was foreshadowed in the pre-Internet era by Stan-ley Kubrick's cinematic masterpiece of 1971, *A Clockwork Orange*, in which a deranged youth, Alex De Large – a forerunner of the apathetic, dangerous young thug today on TikTok – is the central fig-ure in the movie. De Large perpetrates a daily crime spree wantonly and recklessly, foreshadowing the criminal TikTokers of today. The movie ends with no proper resolution. But the scenario of senseless, aimless violence that a teenager can perpetrate is eerily prophetic, as the baby gangs of Italy now confirm. Alex is a goalless and ruthless young person trapped in a weary, decaying environment. His only way out is through intimidation and physicality. He is a ticking time bomb ready to explode at any instant. Alex feels an acute and urgent need to change – indeed to "save" – the world. But he does not know what to save it from. The rage in Alex's eyes is the rage shown by contemporary camorristi. The difference between Alex and TikTok camorristi is that the latter form tribes. Within these, there emerges an implicit set of attitudes, beliefs, values, and principles which define an evanescent self-styled code of honor, subject to constant modification according to generations of camorristi. The social media world provides an illusory sense of invulnerability, at the same time that it instills a view of others as spiteful outsiders.

Social media systems have allowed anyone to interact with anyone else. This has profoundly affected how we now negotiate meaning with each other. As Spanish sociologist Manuel Castells (1996: 500) predicted at the threshold of Web 2.0 world:

> Emergent social structures across domains of human activity and experience leads to an over-arching conclusion: as an historical trend, dominant functions and processes in the Information Age are increasingly organized around networks. Networks constitute the new social morphology of our societies, and the diffusion of networking logic substantially modifies the operation and outcomes in processes of production, experience, power, and culture. While the networking form of social organization has existed in other times and spaces, the new information technology paradigm provides the material basis for its pervasive expansion throughout the entire social structure.

Criminal networks do indeed have a new "social morphology." The term "Mafia" meant distinctiveness in the past, based on a code of honor. This no longer applies. There is little distinction between camorristi and ordinary street gangs. The TikTok criminals and the camorristi seek physical power over others randomly, not according to any code of criminal conduct. Traditional criminal organizations still remain the more dangerous ones, seeking to control territories and officials by expanding their strategies with cyber tools – a trait that makes them increasingly perilous as they constantly adapt to a world that is changing its social morphology daily.

5

FROM MYTHOLOGIES TO MEMETICS AND BEYOND

Prologue

A one-minute TikTok video that went viral in the fall of 2021 showed drug traffickers trying to escape a Spanish Customs Surveillance Service vessel on an inflatable boat yelling screechingly to the boat's pilot to speed up (reported in Suarez, 2021). The video, which received more than one million views, looked like a scene from any drug cartel movie. As such, the video raises two questions encapsulating what criminality has become: Who took the video and why? Why did a one-minute snapshot of a gang go viral? The video is yet another piece of evidence of a trend that characterizes criminality in the smartphone age. Like everyone else today, criminals desire to document their exploits and even routine activities on social media, bragging about the excitement that their criminal lifestyle offers. But the documentation is hardly a permanent one. A few days after, the video was posted, it received almost no new visitors and no new comments. As discussed in the previous chapter, even traditional organized crime groups now record their exploits on social media. Unlike the random gangs that emerge online, however, the traditional ones do not showcase their real criminal operations on social media, just videos of themselves in diverse social situations, as if to create an ongoing filmic narrative of their lives, directed by themselves, instead of a Hollywood director. From the investigative angle, such trends have

DOI: 10.4324/9781003278597-6

entailed a concomitant shift in operations. Because of the threat of criminals using constantly updated technologies, law enforcement has now had to become a highly sophisticated computer-based investigative enterprise. The FBI, for instance, created the Hi-Tech Organized Crime Unit platform, which utilizes new technologies to counteract organized crime, in cooperation with the International Organized Crime Intelligence and Operations Center. The question becomes: Given that technologies change rapidly, how will organized crime and police investigations evolve? Has technology finally obliterated the traditional ways of the mafias, including their reliance on rituals and related myths?

Certainly, the mafias' new generations show a diminished interest in the codes, including allegiance to the founding myths and legends that the older mafiosi told about themselves. In an age of memes and viral videos, these have little resonance. Even the Hollywood-crafted image of the wise guy criminal no longer resonates with the young mafiosi, who are carving out their image online. So, as the myths and codes of the past take on declining value among the younger generations, what will keep the mafias distinctive? Will the age-old image of the mafias as honorable societies finally dissipate into cyberspace? Such questions will be addressed in this final chapter.

Given the adaptability that mafia cultures have always shown, it could well be that there will soon be a new amplification (to use McLuhan's notion), a Mafia 3.0, which utilizes sophisticated technologies, such as artificial intelligence and virtual reality. If so, how will criminal operations be carried out? Will the dualistic character of the Mafia 2.0 also change, or will it expand even more? As discussed throughout this book, mafia-type organizations live in two universes – on the Dark Web where they carry out many, if not most, of their criminal operations and on social media, where they put themselves on public display, no matter what risks this may pose.

Myths Versus Memes

Mafias – from the 'Ndrangheta to the Yakuza and the Triads – have always spun imaginary tales about their origins to legitimize themselves in broader historical–social terms. The stories invariably revolve around a Robin Hood theme, whereby the criminal organizations portray themselves as warriors who emerged from among the oppressed ordinary people themselves, becoming avengers of the social injustices and protectors of the underprivileged classes (Seal, 2009). In this scenario, extortion, for instance, is represented by the mafiosi as a form of fealty for the protection they afford – a kind of reasonable fee for their services. The Robin Hood principle was initially identified by Eric Hobsbawm in his 1959 book *Primitive Rebels*, as a central one for reactionary groups to legitimize their violent actions. Hobsbawm maintained that this was a widespread phenomenon in many societies throughout recorded history in reaction to social injustices. However, the truth is that there is no Robin Hood altruism in any of the traditional criminal organizations. Their emergence was an opportunistic response to social conditions – not a means for rectifying them. They devised and spread myths about themselves to justify their illegal activities and established codes of honor to reinforce their chivalric image further. But as the sheer brutality of the groups terrified the very people that they were purportedly supposed to protect, it was becoming ever more apparent that the chivalric myth was just a convenient story of false legitimization. This story became less relevant to the mobsters themselves as they started migrating to cyberspace where new narrative and symbolic structures emerged to supplant the traditional ones.

A classic example of the latter is the Garduña legend, a pseudo-story told and retold in different versions by the three traditional Italian criminal organizations – the Sicilian Mafia, the Calabrian 'Ndrangheta, and the Neapolitan Camorra. The legend claims that the three "honorable societies" descended directly from three Spanish medieval chivalric knights, called Osso (Bone), Mastrosso (Master Bone), and Carcagnosso (Heel Bone), who belonged to a secret medieval society called Garduña. In 1412, the knights are said to have killed a merciless nobleman who was planning maliciously to violate their sister. After escaping by sea to avoid prison, they became shipwrecked on Favignana (a Mediterranean island near Sicily), where they hid for 29 years. While there, the knights designed a code of honor to become the basis for the conduct of all mafias. When the knights emerged from their hiding place, they migrated to different parts of Italy – Osso went to Sicily to found the Mafia; Mastrosso to Calabria to establish the 'Ndrangheta, and Carcagnosso to Naples to found the Camorra. This story has become part of the folklore of different regions, reimagined in songs and legends. However, no historical evidence exists to substantiate the Garduña legend in any of its versions. It was convenient fiction, meant to create a mystique for the three mafias to emphasize their heroism, honesty, integrity, sense of social justice, and honor. It is a mystique that is imprinted in the word *'Ndrangheta* itself, which comes from a Greek dialect spoken at the time of Homer, meaning "a courageous and valorous man." All the traditional criminal organizations tell similar stories of their origins. The Japanese Yakuza, for instance, see themselves as the descendants of ancient warrior knights who stood up for the common people. Significantly, their self-styled image as honorable warriors with great martial arts skills has been embedded into the popular imagination, as can be seen in the many movies about their exploits, despite their real-life vicious activities against the people they claimed to help.

Mafiosi are hardly folk heroes, but they have always portrayed themselves to be so − a strategy they have used to give them license to torture, murder, and dismember people in their twisted pursuit of justice. But the era of mythology with the chivalric images that such mafias have invented for themselves are hardly translatable to cyberspace, which has all but eliminated the need for such ancient tales. Dark Mafias operate in the darkest regions of cyberspace, where the ancient myths have no meaning. They also inhabit the social media universe, where they boast about themselves by making one-minute videos of their achievements and goals, in place of the traditional oral narrations. A possible consequence of this shift from the pseudo-narratives of the past to the new digital forms of representation is that traditional criminal organizations, which were held together by common origin stories, are now susceptible to a mutation, rather than an evolution. While the myths still exist, they are told in fragmented ways in the form of memetic snippets and personal recollections, which dilutes their cohesiveness in a significant way. In turn, this implies that the sense of unique identity that has always allowed mobsters to set themselves markedly apart from random gangs may have dissipated in cyberspace. If anything, the new generations of criminals rely on memes and viral videos to document their moments in time − which are transitory and hardly collatable into an overall narrative to be passed on to future generations. As a result, the "mythological mafia" has become a "memetic" version of itself, having lost its historically based organicity − a logical consequence of hybrid criminality, as different groups band together in cyberspace to pool resources and using social media to interpret their criminal actions in *sui generis* ways, with little or no connection to any previous mythology or codes of honor.

Foundation myths are powerful cultural tales. Their narrative structure becomes embedded into the collective consciousness of a group, repeated for centuries, serving the function of transmitting the cultural heritage of a group to future generations, helping to create and consolidate its identity and cementing the sense of belonging. Myths emerge to explicate in narrative form the moral, symbolic, and ethical norms that constitute a culture. Intuitively aware of this function of origin mythologies, it is little wonder that the traditional criminal groups have relied so heavily on their legends and codes to ensure their stability and even survival. But in cyberspace, the norms and symbols do not accrue the same meaning. Consider the so-called kiss of death (*il bacio della morte*), the sign supposedly given by a mafioso boss to signal that a member of the crime family has been marked for death, as a result of some perceived betrayal or dishonorable action (Sifakis, 2005: 245–246). It is unclear how this symbol emerged within the Italian mafias. One possibility is that it comes from the movies, specifically from a scene in *The Valachi Papers* (1972) when mobster Vito Genovese kissed informer Joe Valachi to warn him that his betrayal of the family was known and that he would suffer the consequences. Now, the question arises: Is this symbol still used with the same meaning today? A search of social media databases revealed that it no longer has any significance, although we found some ironic uses by several individuals.

Rather than the old symbols, codes, and myths, we found a clear shift to new kinds of symbols and recastings of the older ones. For example, in the past, tattoos were generally shied upon by the Italian mafias. But on social media, they are fully displayed on the bodies of the young mafiosi. As we discovered, some of the designs on the tattoos became memes that went viral not only among members of the same criminal organization, but also among the followers of their social media profiles, becoming a kind of branded identity engraved directly on the skin. An example was the *Love* tattoo that young members of a Camorra clan of the Sanità district in Naples adopted to display on their bodies: the first letter in the word itself is in the shape of a gun, the second a grenade, the third a razor, and the fourth a Kalashnikov. This seemingly has become a symbolic tattoo that anyone can adopt, whether or not they are members of a criminal gang, as a sign of violence, turning the notion of *love* on its head. In effect, there is no symbolic exclusivity restricted to members of criminal organizations, as there was in the past. Mafia symbols are created on a daily basis online and can be adopted by anyone, as a fashion statement, rather than connected to any code of honor. Other tattooing trends that we discovered among young camorristi include the following: tattoos of the names of deceased criminal friends; religious images; images taken from different popular cultures, such as tattoos of the Joker (the villain of the Batman comic fame); and tattoos paying homage to dictator Benito Mussolini, considered a "great boss" of the past who conquered enemies of the people. The earliest example of Mussolini symbolism is traced to an August 26, 2015, Facebook post by the late camorrista Ciro Marfè, who uploaded a photo portraying the dictator in uniform while clenching his fist. On April 11, 2016, Marfè then posted the image of a marble slab on which Mussolini's aphorism is engraved: "We do not want war, but we do not fear it." The dictator theme is a common one in online symbolism. Walter Mallo, a young boss of the Miano district, posted a famous statement by dictator Fidel Castro, "¡Patria o Muerte, Venceremos!" ("Our country or death, we will conquer!") on February 7, 2016, which went viral. Such symbols are metaphors of power that a criminal wants to convey. But they are hardly organic ones. They evolve through cyberspace as memes that are reassembled over and over by followers of the social media sites, who adopt them for a while as part of personal branding but which evanesce into cyberspace in a short period time. Overall, we found no evidence that today's young mobsters are embracing the old myths. Instead, they are creating their own symbolism and stories, which, however, have a short shelf life, unlike the mythologies of the past, which have persisted since they were concocted.

The term *meme,* as mentioned before, was introduced by evolutionary scholar Richard Dawkins in his book, *The Selfish Gene* (1976), to explain how nongenetic information is transmitted from individual to individual and from generation to generation. For Dawkins, memes are not just metaphors for such traditional concepts as "ideas," "words," "symbols," and so on; they are as real as genes, so he asserts. In effect, memes are to the mind what genes are to the body. Whatever the theory's validity, this term has emerged as an apt one in Internet culture, where memes (a cover term for words, symbols, videos, and so on) appear in great abundance daily and disappear just as quickly into the void of cyberspace. Unlike Dawkins's original theory, which envisions memes as psycho-biological units programmed into the brain by biology, which are directive of cultural evolution, gaining permanence in subsequent generations, Internet memes are characterized by virality, immediacy, and ephemerality. They are short-lived because of the pastiche nature of their mutation in cyberspace, whereby a meme at any stage in its individualized modification as it spreads can be understood only if one has access to its immediate previous forms (Wiggins, 2019).

The central question here concerns the implications that the shift from mythic to memetic mafia culture might bear: Will the one-minute video of the drug cartel or the Camorra *love* tattoo posts resonate with subsequent generations of criminals or even with the same criminal organizations the next day? Can memetic structures, which document a specific moment in time, cohere into an overarching narrative of mafia achievement that can be passed on to subsequent generations? In the traditional world of the mafias, codes, symbols, and mythic texts were designed to provide continuity to a clan, transcending the immediacy of fleeting trends. To use linguist Ferdinand de Saussure's (1916) apt term, they lack diachronicity – a natural, historical mechanism connecting them to other referential domains of history within a system. A memetically based self-perpetuating diachronic historiography is an oxymoron. History requires events, episodes, and symbols to coalesce into an organic narration, such as the Garduña one; without this, the group will be cut off from the past.

Mafias may no longer have a choice but to use memetic forms to chart their ongoing history, whatever that may look like, given the hyperreal mindset of people in the Internet Age. As Ryan M. Milner (2016) has argued and amply illustrated, memes are now a lingua franca, collectively created and transformed by users across vast digital networks. It is impossible to imagine a significant cultural moment that does not produce a constellation of memetic texts that comment on it via limitless iterations. However, Milner suggests that this does occur because the important memes (to a group) are gradually woven into larger discourses. For better or worse, Milner remarks, these will merge into their form of historiography that will be transmitted to subsequent generations via sites that collect memes that have broad significance. Extending this to mafias, the suggestion is that, as the current generations chronicle their achievements and ideas memetically, they will purportedly be passed on through digital channels, rather than by word of mouth or by the printed word. Digital institutions such as *Know Your Meme* and *Encyclopedia Dramatica*, among others, are now meme databases from which events can be reconstructed. History is no longer written as a continuous time-binding narrative but as a memetic amalgam of moments that will be interpreted randomly, by the next generations.

All this raises several problems that may have escaped the enthusiasm of meme historians. One of these is the subjectivity that will characterize the memetic forms of the future. However, as Milner suggests, since meme websites contain a "deluge of context," readers can be trusted to come to sage and logical conclusions about the historical relevance of memes and memetic discourses. In other words, history will be in the hands of future generations who will be tasked to make sense of the memes. A historical narrative is constructed in such a way as to represent a sequence of events or actions that are felt to be logically connected to each other or causally intertwined in some way. Of course, the selection of the events is a subjective one on the part of the historian; but consensus is reached when various narratives about the same events are compared, so that a common ground of understanding can be extrapolated from them.

Stories keep historically established values meaningful; it is unlikely that memetic discourses will do the same. The memetic historiography of today's organized criminals, if it will truly be passed on to ensure their sustainability, will be a narrativeless, image-based, fragmentary presentation of moments in time. On the Internet, ideas go viral if they are catchy and relevant socially but quickly become extinct if they fall out of step with the contemporaneity of interests. Memes capture these momentary fragments of interest, and presumably, these will be glued narratively together by subsequent generations. But how will the memetic bits be put together to create a picture of what truly happened and what it meant? Clearly, the shift from myths to memes has definite implications for the future that are profound and far-reaching. While criminal operations will certainly exist and even expand, the cultural structures of the criminal organizations may become insignificant; however, without these there are no mafias as such, just gangs with computer skills.

A Dualistic Character

In addition to the ephemerality factor that defines a "memetic mafia," another counteractive factor likely to change its nature from the past is the dualistic character of the new generations, as discussed throughout. To reiterate here, the dualism is a result of the world of the matrix, whereby the mafioso inhabits two digital spaces – the Dark

Web marketplaces and other sites in which he situates his criminal operationality, and the social media platforms which he uses to present himself to the world in ways that would have led to his elimination by the clan in the past, because it would have been seen not only as foolish behavior for a man of honor but also as imperiling the very operationality of the mafias. Organized crime thrives in the shadows, away from the public gaze, minimizing its profile, not amplifying it. That is hardly the case today, when just the opposite holds – braggadocio and showing off are expected from both the mafiosi and their followers, no matter the consequences.

The paradox of this paradigm shift has been a subtheme of this book. While the dark side of the dualistic character operates in the shadows of cyberspace and is more powerful and sinister than ever; the cool side is involved in open defiance of the mafias' age-old norms, engaging in public online insults, profane language, and posting videos of crimes that often go viral. This has created a rupture in the unity of the traditional mafias. Ironically, even the older mafia aristocracy uses social media to some extent, although it keeps away from the kind of memetic exposure in which the younger criminals revel. Clearly, the code of the *uomini d'onore* of the past may have been shattered by cyberspace (in some part). The new generations are *uomini di TikTok*, as they can be called. Some operational aspects of the past remain solidly in place, including the engagement in political corruption, which is still integral to the functioning of the younger mafias, as is violence and threats of violence. But the dualistic character of the young mafioso has no counterpart in the history of mafias, when both criminal operationality and everyday conduct and behavior were seen as organically intertwined (Leukfeldt et al., 2017).

Explaining the rise of the new mafiosi requires a technology-based criminological framework. In our view, the theory of the simulacrum in particular is the one that provides relevant insights, since it might explain how and why the dualistic nature of mafiosi today is a product of technology and a factor in disrupting the unity and hegemony of mafia structure intentionally, rendering it more apt to dissipate. The simulacrum effect, as mentioned, refers to the fact that communicating through computer screens impels us to see what occurs on the other side of the screen just as meaningful as what occurs in reality, whereby a simulacrum is formed between the two. Baudrillard (Chapter 1) argued that the simulacrum directly affects cognition, whereby what happens on the screen becomes as important, if not more so, than what happens in reality. Mobsters, like everyone else, have been subjected to the simulacrum, impelling them to live on and through the screen where, they seem to believe, their criminal lives assume new meaning, as they broaden their reach both within the clan and outside of it through followers and fans. Daily contact through the screen is as important as contact in the real world. Simulacrum theory might explain why the myths of the past have given way to ephemeral memes – the former emerged in real space spread through the spoken and written word; the latter exist in hyperreality, where the spoken word has become a memetic word, constantly morphing as it spreads across social media platforms. In summary, the simulacrum effect has changed the nature of organized crime in the span of a decade or so. Consider, for example, the definition of organized crime included in the turn-of-the Millennium report of the United Nations Office on Drugs and Crime (2004), which stressed that to qualify as a criminal organization it must have a geographical locus and continuity of its membership. Barely a decade after, this definition was revised since geography became no longer a factor in the constitution of an organized criminal group, which can spring up entirely online. The continuity requirement has also become attenuated, given the frequent turnover of young mobsters. Of course, some individuals are still considered essential to the conduct and stability of the group and its operations, while others are deemed nonessential, maybe even expendable. As discussed, the new hierarchies show a similar structure to the past ones, with a leadership at the top and foot soldiers at the bottom. But the addition of computer-savvy individuals has changed the perception of what a hierarchy entails, given that membership is not as strictly controlled as it was in the past.

The dualistic character has also made traditional mafias more susceptible to exposure to the authorities – a fact contributing to the destabilization of organized crime as understood traditionally. Since the mid-2010s, agencies such as the FBI, Interpol, Scotland Yard, Europol, the Italian police, and many others have strategically developed their counter-technologies to intercept and locate criminal communications, both in Dark Web and surface web systems. The example of Anom (Chapter 1) is just one of the many devices that are now developed and used by the authorities as part of counterintelligence and cyber-sting operations. Recall here that the Anom communication network gave the police access to thousands of encrypted messages of numerous criminal syndicates operating in over 100 countries, allowing them to take down global organized criminals, drug trafficking gangs, and money laundering organizations, regardless of where they operated geographically. But, as also discussed, this has not stopped the mafiosi from finding new ways of using technology to both perpetrate crimes and shield themselves from persecution. In 2020, the EncroChat-encrypted platform was dismantled by the Operational Taskforce EMMA (as discussed), followed in 2021 by another takedown of a similar nature, which successfully blocked the further use of encrypted communications by organized crime networks via the so-called Sky ECC communication service tool. But such successes have hardly discouraged criminals from finding other ways of conducting secret operations, as we have discussed throughout this book.

Another theoretical paradigm that might be used for explaining the current mafias is meme theory. In moving away from traditional myths to ephemeral memetic stories, mafias may be undergoing a truly radical cultural reimagination of themselves. The Polish-born British anthropologist Bronislaw Malinowski (1922) argued that cultures came about so that humans could solve similar physical and moral problems the world over in creative and imaginative ways. He claimed that the words, symbols, codes, rituals, and institutions that humans have created, no matter how strange they might at first seem, had a universal function – to solve similar life problems, through the expressive and intellectual activities that these forms allow. It is difficult to envision what kinds of "problems," to use Malinowski's terminology, meme culture aims to solve. Memes are not problem-solving structures; nor are they time capsules. They will likely become meaningless as time progresses. This has implications: Will the mafias disappear in the electronic fog of cyberspace, or will they emerge as new structures, adapting to the ever-changing world of technology, as implied by McLuhan's laws of media?

Mafia 3.0

Indications are that mafia criminality will survive, mainly because it is adaptive, responding opportunistically to changes in society and technology. The criminal groups understand now, as never before, that they cannot stay away from broader cultural trends. A gang like the Hells Angels attained fame, not because of their brutal exploits, but because of the movies and other media exploiting their outlaw culture as entertainment. In a world where technological advancements enable the police to identify and track criminal organizations globally, a gang such as the Hells Angels has had to become increasingly expert at how to use technologies for self-serving purposes, as we saw with the gang's use of Facebook against the Winnipeg hotel that initially refused to allow them to stay there. The lesson here is that, as the technologies change, organized crime will change accordingly.

Movies and television series continue to portray nostalgically the wise guy mafioso – a construction of American popular culture. The new mafiosi are different, having adapted to the world of the matrix. The lure of criminal societies will endure, not because of economic conditions but because of the power, fame, and fortune that criminal lifestyles promise to some young people. Moreover, the mafias' ability to stay up-to-date with new technologies has become an attractive trait for recruiting members. There is little doubt that it has started to enter the worlds of AI and virtual reality (VR) – a fact that is leading to yet another version of organized criminality, which can be called the Mafia 3.0 – an adaptation to the anticipated Web 3.0 world, which is just around the corner. The Web 1.0 was a static information provider where people read websites but rarely interacted with them; the Web 2.0 is an interactive, social network system that allows collaboration between users; and the Web 3.0 will change both how websites are made and how people interact within them. The Mafia 3.0 will undoubtedly become increasingly dependent for its survival on AI. A website using what is now called Augmented AI can provide the data a hacker is seeking automatically and even suggest what else he can extract from a site. All this means that the Mafia 3.0 will have an even more decentralized structure, which will enable it to operate in highly automated ways.

Another area that the Mafia 3.0 will enter into is virtual reality (VR), a computer-simulated, three-dimensional environment designed to appear and render the feeling of being immersed in a real environment. The VR world creates a veritable simulacrum of reality – an engagement with imaginary worlds as if they were real worlds. People using VR equipment can look around the simulated world, move around, and interact with features or items. As a result, the difference between reality and imaginary worlds becomes a true simulacrum. Already in 1979, the military and other governmental agencies realized the importance of adopting the emerging VR technology for military and training purposes. In a Web 3.0 world, VR will make it routine for people to present themselves to others and interact with them as holograms. Studies have shown that, after a while, the simulation affects people emotionally as in real life (Lavoie et al., 2021).

In a pivotal study on "AI-Enabled Future Crime," Caldwell et al. (2020) discuss the implications of AI for the future of criminality and for the organizational structure of criminal groups, which in the case of the Mafia 3.0 would involve the allocation of new roles and duties to AI specialists and psychologists. A jointly developed report by Europol, the United Nations Interregional Crime and Justice Research Institute, and Trend Micro looking into current and predicted criminal uses of AI (Europol, 2021) provides the following insight that is of relevance here:

> AI promises the world greater efficiency, automation and autonomy. At a time where the public is getting increasingly concerned about the possible misuse of AI, we have to be transparent about the threats, but also look into the potential benefits from AI technology. This report will help us not only to anticipate possible malicious uses and abuses of AI, but also to prevent and mitigate those threats proactively. This is how we can unlock the potential AI holds and benefit from the positive use of AI systems.

The report goes on to emphasize that cybercriminals will leverage AI both as an attack and surface vector. The former refers to a method or scenario that can be exploited to present fake information as indistinguishable from facts. An example is the use of video "deepfakes," or videos of a person whose face or body has been digitally altered so that they appear to be someone else. Deepfakes have already been used as part of social engineering scams, fooling people into thinking they are receiving instructions from a trusted individual. A surface vector refers to a software environment wherein an unauthorized user can enter or extract data. Such technology opens up a vast new marketplace for hybrid criminality to thrive. Cybercriminals are actually using AI already to carry out large-scale social engineering attacks, making them more efficient. As the Europol report warns, criminals' AI systems are being developed to enhance the effectiveness of malware and to disrupt anti-malware and facial recognition systems. While in the past social engineering scams had to be tailored to specific targets, through AI, they can be deployed massively.

One area into which the mafias are already moving is the world of the so-called virtual economy, which is an economic system existing in cyberspace involving the exchange of virtual goods in the context of massively multiplayer online games. People enter these virtual economies for recreation and entertainment rather than necessity. However, some also interact within the virtual economies for economic benefit (Castronova, 2014). The proliferation of virtual currencies in such VR worlds has created an attractive financial reason for international organized crime groups to enter into them, given that organized criminals can create computer malware and social engineering scams to specifically locate and target large numbers of potential gaming victims. While one can certainly argue whether "virtual crimes" constitute "real crimes," there is no doubt about the economic or psychological effect that these crimes have on their victims, since these virtual spaces are every bit as real to their visitors as is the physical world. In summary, as AI and related systems evolve, the mafias will undoubtedly evolve along with them, becoming even darker, hiding in the virtual worlds that AI makes possible. It remains to be seen how the cool guy mafioso will fit into this simulacrum universe; our guess is that he (and she) will learn quickly how to use new technological tools for self-promotion, ostentation, and other vainglorious reasons. The advent of the Internet offered new opportunities for the mobsters. The growing fields of AI and VR will offer newer opportunities that the Mafia 3.0 will likely exploit. As the Europol (2021) report concluded:

> The promise of more efficient automation and autonomy is inseparable from the different schemes that malicious actors are capable of. Criminals and organized crime groups have been swiftly integrating new technologies into their *modi operandi*.

The era of AI will finally signal the end of the fascination with the "mythic mafias" of the past. The myths of the past have already evanesced into cyberspace; with the expansion of an algorithm society, they will undoubtedly disappear. AI has already changed everyone's life, including the lives of mobsters who use it in the same ways legitimate companies do. Distribution of illicit drugs, counterfeit goods, and illegal weapons is increasingly being coordinated by those with the ability to use algorithms effectively. The Mafia 3.0 may already be here.

Case Studies: V

The case studies here illustrate how the shift in organized crime has been occurring in specific ways, including how AI is starting to become a part of criminal operations. They show, as well, how law enforcement has had to adapt to the chameleon nature of the mobsters. One of the previous case studies is revisited in the context of its implications for the shift away from previous models of mafioso culture to present-day ones. Case studies such as these offer concrete snapshots of how McLuhan's global village is shaping life and how it will guide the future of social interactions. As McLuhan (1962: 35) put it: "The human family now exists under conditions of a global village. We live in a single constricted space resonant with tribal drums." The criminals live in that same constricted space and are hearing the same drums – to extend McLuhan's metaphor.

The growing technological complexity of organized criminality calls for a rethinking of the conceptual approaches to organized crime itself – hence they need to adopt theories such as the simulacrum. As Fernández-Planells and Orduña-Malea (2021: 2099) discovered in their review of the relevant literature, it is becoming ever more apparent that technology is the channel through which modern societies now evolve, a fact which poses "challenges, risks and recommendations for future social media research."

Case Study: Sky Global

Sky Global was a communications network and service provider founded in 2008, with headquarters in Vancouver, Canada. The company was suspected of providing criminals who were primarily involved in drug trafficking with secure messaging applications and phones that had the ability to self-destruct messages, secure audio messages, and an app that could disguise itself as a calculator. Sky Global constitutes a prototypical case in point of how criminal organizations adopt evolving technology systems opportunistically. In 2021, the authorities dismantled the company with a series of raids against the criminal organizations that were using its services in several countries after the U.S. Department of Justice had issued an arrest warrant against the company's CEO and the FBI had seized its website. One of the company's main selling points to organized criminals was that it did not store encrypted messages on its servers. Its website promoted this:

> If your contact is not reachable (for example if their device is off), we hold the encrypted message for up to 48 hours, then delete it. If they do not read it in that time frame, the message cannot be retrieved.

Ironically, the investigators had intercepted about one million encrypted messages, which provided a clear picture of the workings of the criminal organizations that did business with the website, including their global reach, their financial resources, and their criminal activities. The Sky Global case was one of many that afforded investigators insights into transnational criminality in the global village. One of the most interesting aspects of the case was that big data was key to the investigation's success, constituting a feature of the Internet that the criminals could not step away from. This consists in large datasets that AI machine-learning systems can analyze to reveal patterns, trends, and associations. Such systems are now standard in police operations because of their ability to detect patterns instantly (Brayne, 2017). Once caught by an algorithm, there is no way to snake one's way out of the situation via subterfuge or intimidation. The algorithm cannot be intimidated.

In a way, the dark mafias have become entangled in their crimes, incapable of detaching themselves from them. The Sky Global case showed that the gangsters, like everyone else, now live in an environment in which AI devices are installed in everyday objects. The key to understanding the emergence of a potential Mafia 3.0 lies in understanding how AI technologies will evolve, and how these will allow the organized criminal groups to conduct their operations ever more efficiently and broadly.

Case Study: Alyssa Navarro

The case of Alyssa Navarro (reported in Brewster, 2022) brought out how the mafias are now tapping into the use of technologies, such as online video gaming, to enact some of their traditional tasks. In particular, the Navarro case showed how the drug cartels use popular games to recruit meth mules. The game in question was Grand Theft Auto which features fictional games allowing users to pretend to be working for a Mexican cartel. As this case showed, however, the same game also provided real-life cartel recruiters, who similarly played the game, a locus to utilize for recruiting players for real-life criminal work. In 2021, the Mexican police discovered that drug cartels were in fact recruiting young video game players over Grand Theft Auto Online. However, they lacked concrete evidence to make arrests.

A break came shortly after when American authorities had gathered evidence that the videogame was a recruitment instrument for the narcotics cartels. It started when Customs and Border Protection officials in Arizona inspected a Jeep Cherokee, finding a massive stash of methamphetamines in the vehicle. The driver, Alyssa Navarro, claimed that she had been playing Grand Theft Auto Online in January when she met a gaming platform man who called himself "George." After forming a friendship with the individual within the confines of the game, Navarro affirmed that she then started talking to him on Snapchat, later meeting him in person in Phoenix. George had asked her over Snapchat whether she would like to make some money as a "runner" for electronics, so that they could be sold in Mexico. He had promised her up to 2,000 dollars per trip, depending on how big the load was. Investigators obtained the Snapchat messages from Navarro's phone which showed George promising "a lot of money" and offering her the use of a truck, which turned out to be the Jeep in which she was apprehended. Navarro claimed that she was told to meet a contact in Mexico called "Alfredo," who gave her the Jeep, which she was to fill with gas only at certain gas stations along the way, taking the vehicle to another unidentified individual. Navarro claimed innocence, and even though she admitted that the whole thing seemed strange; she still went ahead and met her mysterious contact.

Similar recruitment events have occurred throughout the world of organized crime. As Brewster (2022) remarks:

> Computer games have proven increasingly popular for other kinds of grooming. The explosion in the popularity of online gaming has led to platforms like Minecraft, XBox Live, or games like GTA Online and Fortnite becoming spots where many children spend time with existing friends and make new ones. The anonymity of an online gaming handle has, however, attracted predators, and the Justice Department has prosecuted multiple men who tried to hide behind online personas to coerce minors.

In another strikingly similar 2021 case, security officials reported an arrest of three young people in Mexico's southern state of Oaxaca as they boarded a bus after having been promised payment to work as police lookouts in the country's north. An online recruiter had offered 8,000 pesos for every half-month of work through the mobile battle royale game Free Fire.

Videogame technology has also been central in various police operations. For instance, the FBI pulled videogame data to break up a cocaine ring in 2019 (reported in Hall, 2019). The case occurred in Missouri involving a cocaine dealer who orchestrated crimes using chat services on PlayStation 4, Xbox One, and Nintendo Switch. A search warrant stated that a certain Curtis Alexander was involved in a "multi-kilogram level" cocaine deal. An online sting operation discovered the perpetrator – an FBI source requested nine ounces of cocaine via the PS4 messaging client. Curtis believed that in-game voice communication was more secure than text chat and asked that the transaction continue "during the game."

Case Study: The Casamonica Case Redux

As discussed in Chapter 2, this case is a significant one, showing how the Dark Mafia has evolved, bringing out the implications of this evolution. It concerns the Casamonica clan, operating in the Lazio region, with ties to the 'Ndrangheta, the Sacra Corona Unita, and the Camorra. It had little public exposure until a lavish funeral for crime boss Vittorio Casamonica in 2015 exposed him and his clan to both the public and the authorities. The subsequent operation to take down the clan netted millions of euros and hundreds of arrests. All this was made possible because of the clan's online operations in Italy, Spain, Germany, Lithuania, Ireland, and the U.K. The criminals had run spear phishing email campaigns that duped victims into sending money to certain bank accounts. After the mobsters received the ill-gotten gains, they laundered the currency through front companies, money mules, and cryptocurrency methods. The investigators discovered that the large criminal network had a pyramid structure, including several specialized computer-based roles.

This case is a prototypical one for grasping concretely how previously traditional organized criminals now operate in cyberspace. First, the criminal operations were not the work of a single group; there was a collaboration among various criminal organizations in the network. Second, hybrid criminality was involved, whereby online and offline operations were coordinated and synchronized. In addition to cybercrimes, those arrested were also charged with traditional crimes, such as assault, illegal possession of weapons, and murder. Third, mobsters and accomplices used emerging technologies and employed individuals with computer skills to help them carry out crimes such as voice phishing, in which the criminals tricked victims over the phone into coughing up personal information, and SIM-swapping schemes, whereby they persuaded phone service providers to transfer victims' phone numbers to another device to access accounts. The raid, named Fontana-Almabahía (Chapter 2), also revealed how law enforcement now approaches organized criminality, using the same kind of technology as the criminals, collaboratively with investigators from Europol and the Italian and Spanish national police.

Perhaps, the most relevant aspect of this case is that it showed that the Italian mafias had entered the twentieth-first century, cooperating online and offline with other criminal syndicates for mutual benefit. The mobsters kidnapped a woman, holding her at gunpoint, and taking her to an unknown location to force her to hand over all her money – a violent action involving a woman that went largely unnoticed. Europol's assessment of the Casamonica operation encapsulates how organized crime has evolved in the Millennium, calling the hackers and criminals "a single organized crime group," not a pastiche of multiple groups.

The apparent willingness of Italian crime families to update their operations by engaging in hybrid criminality does not mean that they have completely given up their old ways – the outer concentric circle of our model (Chapter 3) is still somewhat influential in shaping the character of the current mafias. This became evident during the COVID-19 crisis in 2020, when mobsters resorted to their tried-and-tested methods, taking advantage of people's economic difficulties, offering food and other support so as to exact future favors or take over entire territories. Old habits die hard, to cite a common saying. The older mafiosi are still holding on to their past as much as they can. Still, it is also becoming apparent that the new generations are leaving the past more and more behind, out of necessity to adapt (or else fade away). Having grown up in the age of the matrix, they now know no other reality than the world of Web 2.0 society.

Case Study: The Mafia 3.0

A Cave Automatic Virtual Environment (CAVE) is an immersive virtual reality environment that allows investigators to portray different situations in the simulated space. In South Wales in 2018, the Gwent police became the first agency to use CAVE technology to train the police in tackling crimes in the Web 3.0 society that is crystallizing. Similar tools are being developed worldwide to fight what has been called the Mafia 3.0 here.

The Netherlands police forces have been particularly active in this area, collaborating with computer scientists, systems engineers, and design professionals on various crime-fighting projects. One such project, *CSI: The Hague*, can digitize the evidence at crime scenes, which it then passes on to an AI program to create a virtual version of the crime scene so that forensic investigators could revisit it whenever it was necessary to do so. Another project, called *On the Spot*, has allowed the Port of Rotterdam police and the fire brigade to train collaboratively in virtual forensic investigations. As the Mafia 3.0 grows, it is ever more obvious that crime and technology can no longer be seen as separate evolving entities. Europol's 2021 report warned, in fact, that organized crime groups are now trying to stay ahead of the authorities, becoming more and more adept at using AI to spread their global reach and to render their operations maximally efficient. As the Gwen Police example highlights, the biggest challenge is to detect and investigate incidents so as to predict activities and react to them effectively.

Artificial intelligence (AI) is swiftly fueling the development of the Mafia 3.0. Together with machine learning – a subfield of AI that analyzes large volumes of data to find patterns via algorithms – enterprising criminal groups are now immersed in technologies that help them refine and expand the scope and scale of their operations. Through AI, organized cyber groups can automate the first steps of a planned attack through content generation, improve their intelligence gathering, and speed up the rate at which potential victims can be compromised. AI-powered drones now even allow criminals to replace human mules since these can carry drugs, money, or other criminal materials to specified locations by remote control.

Case Study: The Future Is Here

For centuries, the basic pattern involved in organized criminality consisted of a victim paying extortion money to a boss directly in order to avoid any form of retaliation. Called a protection fee, the fact was that the fee was meant to protect the victim from the extortionist himself, who would pocket the money, as he falsely promised to ensure the continuing safety of the victim. Now, let us shift the scene to the contemporary world of the matrix. Here, the victim receives the extortion request, not from a person who can be identified physically, but from an anonymous entity, via a phishing scam. Identifying the extortionist is virtually impossible. In effect, how would a victim be able to identify an algorithm extorting him? The future is already here, since this is happening frequently. The Mafia 3.0 is becoming darker and darker through technology, as it hides not only in dark spaces on the Internet but in the anonymity of algorithms.

Epilogue

Recalling former Sicilian Prosecutor Roberto Scarpinato's (2015: 129) characterization of the Mafia as an evil that exists "inside us," and extending his metaphor, the question becomes: Can we finally exorcise that evil once and for all, given the sophistication of law enforcement today? As we have attempted to argue in this book, it is unlikely to happen simply because the mafias have adapted to technological change and even kept a bit ahead of such change.

Ironically, mobsters now hide in the dark regions of cyberspace but also expose themselves on social media to which they have become addicted. But they persist, gaining experience in the new technologies, from AI to VR, and likely to evolve into a new version of themselves, called here the Mafia 3.0. The mafiosi are criminal chameleons who know how to adapt to and co-opt changing social and technological systems. There is no exorcism on the horizon; if it is to come, it must begin by making crime culture appear meaningless, or boring, to younger generations. Solutions may involve the counter-use of technologies such as VR to show and impress upon developing minds that there are other ways to gain excitement in the world of the matrix, which does not involve criminality. However, this type of reverse psychology approach has failed in the past and might fail again.

Maybe the dualistic character of Dark Mafia that has crystallized today might ultimately be its Achilles heel allowing for its ultimate dissipartion. Already in the 1990s, the Sicilian Mafioso, Antonino Calderone, emphasized that the Mafia has always been

> a universe doubled, schizophrenic and hallucinated, in which everyone is at the same time friends and enemies of all, in which

everyone professes and flaunts intense loyalty and fidelity, knot and dissolve pacts and federations, at the same time as they claim the false, promote deception, plan conspiracies and ambushes, betray and kill loved ones. And it dominates all the continuous, Hobbesian fear and the danger of violent death.

(Arlacchi, 1993: v)

The world that Calderone describes has not disappeared; it has become even more prevalent in cyberspace, where the "schizophrenic" personality of mobsters, as he called it, has coalesced into a new dualistic form. This hybrid mafia operates in the dark regions of cyberspace but exposes itself vainly on social media platforms to brag about the very conquests gained in those regions. Nonetheless, this has proven insufficient to bring the whole apparatus of organized criminality down. If nothing else, the shift from the Mafia 1.0 to the Mafia 2.0 and the Mafia 3.0 shows that the rigid, hierarchical organizational models that are ascribed to traditional organized crime have become transient and fluid, posing even more challenges to law enforcement and making it virtually impossible to dismantle the whole architecture of organized criminality that inhabits many regions of cyberspace.

So is there any way to break the evolutionary cycle of organized crime? Dismantling the allure of criminal behavior involves, in our view, an analysis of how societies evolve through technology – and this takes us back to McLuhan. The overarching idea in his writings was a simple yet penetrating one – as technology changes, so too do societies, and there is no turning back the clock. The reason is that our tools are extensions of ourselves. Any significant change in how we communicate through technology entails a paradigm shift in cultural systems. As McLuhan himself often intimated, we must come to recognize the negative by-products of technology to contravene them. Perhaps, a day will come when technology will make criminality irrelevant; or on the other hand may spread it everywhere. What is certain is that to keep ahead of the criminal organizations, one must keep an eye on technology and the social practices and motivations that it brings about.

The spread of AI and its co-option by organized criminals may contain the seeds of a potential solution. If the criminals feel that they are under surveillance by a non-sentient entity, all day and all night, they will have to change their *modi operandi* drastically. In so doing, they may have to completely shed the skeins of all previous forms of organized crime. As the TikToker phenomenon involving random criminal gangsterism shows, the organicity of previous forms of organized crime may already be starting to cede to random thuggery, which would be the death knell of *omertà* once and for all. Law enforcement would then have to deal with criminal wantonness rather than dark mafiosi enclaves working in tandem with confreres in cyberspace. The resilience and cleverness of mobsters cannot be underestimated, however. The future may indeed make no distinction between random and organized crime, but the latter will undoubtedly develop strategies to remain somewhat unified. Otherwise it will dissipate into algorithmic programs (Frey, 2017).

In the end, answering the questions raised in this book would be an idealistic venture. We can focus more practically on the technology-crime nexus, so as to see how it evolves. As McLuhan predicted, new technologies, created with all the best intentions, will be used against us at some point. As cybercrime escalates, we actually "run the risk of having our social structures deteriorate into invisible mafia-style communities with the blackmailers ruling the blackmailees," as futurist Thomas Frey (2017) has remarked. Will organized criminals, like everyone else, soon use robots to carry out physical tasks, such as violence and the collection of extortion money? Will they use increasingly sophisticated drones, hacker psycho-bots, and even "brain hackers," to carry out their operations? Territorial criminality is locatable, but virtual-algorithmic crime is not. As Frey (2017) goes on to comment, there is little doubt that a sophisticated organized criminal system is evolving, with unwitting people engaged on multiple levels, not knowing the exact nature of the activities in which they are involved:

> Battlefields of the future will continue to morph along with our tech cultures, and many of the weapons of the future will be unrecognizable by today's standards. In much the same way we never want to show up with a knife for a gunfight, our police forces are a terrible match for tomorrow's criminal undergrounds. We are a long ways from having the right tools and tech needed to deal with tomorrow's criminal enterprises.

Our foray through the tentacles of the Dark Mafia has been intended as a warning about organized crime's ability to evolve, exploiting technology for self-serving purposes. As human social interactions increasingly migrate from real to virtual spaces, so will the panoply of social ills and harms. Given the complexity of the issues involved, the whole assessment and discussion of organized crime must embrace interdisciplinarity concretely, from the study of myths to how AI and robotics are used. But some things never change – indeed, what seems to guarantee the effectiveness of criminality is its ability to instill fear in victims (Ceccato and Nalla, 2020). That fear conveyed in the Black Hand era has become even more intense in cyberspace. The Dark Mafia will become even "darker," hiding in algorithms and simulated representational spaces. As David Tal (2020) has aptly observed:

> Whether it's smuggling drugs and knockoff goods, sneaking refugees across borders, or trafficking women and children, when economies enter into recessions, when nations collapse . . . and when regions suffer devastating environmental disasters, that's when the logistics faculties of criminal organizations thrive. The days of the small-time criminal are numbered. Be it traditional crimes or cybercrimes, they will all become far too risky and the gains far too minimal. For this reason, the remaining individuals with the motivation, propensity, and skillset for crime will likely turn to employment with criminal organizations who have the infrastructure necessary to reduce the costs and risks associated of most forms of criminal activity.

As we discovered in our interviews with police investigators, it is by better understanding the social structures of emerging random street gangs – such as the TikTokers discussed in this book – that we can better psychologically deconstruct the reasons why such criminality is attractive and spreading. In Italy, a group of software engineers has created a centralized, user-friendly, real-time, national database of all goods confiscated by the authorities from the Mafia. This database is now used to coordinate enforcement activities against their country's many mafia-type organizations. At the same time, law enforcement agencies around the word are getting a better understanding of the influence of new technologies on organized crime. Perhaps, as Tal (2020) suggests, technology will ultimately defeat the technology-savvy mafioso, echoing in a modern way Niccolò Machiavelli's observation that deception is needed to defeat the deceiver:

> The new tech will substantially bring down the costs of investigating complex criminal organizations and make it easier to prosecute them. In fact, by 2040, the surveillance and analytics tech that will become available to the police will make running a traditional, centralized criminal organization next to impossible. The only variable, as always seems to be the case, is whether a country has enough uncorrupted politicians and police chiefs willing to use these tools to put an end to these organizations once and for all.

REFERENCES

Adams, J. (2016). *Canada and Cyber. Canadian Global Affairs Institute.* http://
cfcollegefoundation.ca/wp-content/uploads/2016/08/Canada-and-
Cyber-John-Adams-CGAI-2016.pdf.

Adams, T. L., and Smith, S. A. (2008). *Electronic Tribes: The Virtual Worlds of
Geeks, Gamers, Shamans, and Scammers.* Austin: University of Texas Press.

Anderson, L. (2017). Snuff: Murder and Torture on the Internet, and the People
Who Watch It, *The Verge*, June 13, www.theverge.com/2012/6/13/3076557/
snuff-murder-torture-internet-people-who-watch-it.

Anselmi, A. (2019). *Onion Routing, Cripto-valute e Crimine Organizzato.* Pisa:
Pacini.

Arghire, I. (2019). Authorities Takedown GozNym Cybercrime Group That
Stole an Estimated $100 Million, *Security Week*, May 16, www.secu-
rityweek.com/authorities-takedown-goznym-cybercrime-group-stole-
estimated-100-million.

Arlacchi, P. (1993). *Men of Dishonor: Inside the Sicilian Mafia. An Account of
Antonino Calderone.* New York: William Morrow.

Barghout, C. (2018). Manitoba Hells Angels Target Businesses by Posting
1-star Reviews, *CBC*, April 10, www.cbc.ca/news/canada/manitoba/
manitoba-hells-angels-business-reviews-1.4608271.

Barthes, R. (1957). *Mythologies.* Paris: Seuil.

Bartlett, J. (2016). *The Dark Net: Inside the Digital Underworld.* London: Mel-
ville House.

Baudrillard, J. (1981). *Simulacra and Simulations.* Ann Arbor: University of
Michigan Press.

Baudrillard, J. (1983). *Simulations.* New York: Semiotexte.

Behar, R. (2020). Wiseguys Know Pizza: Two Former Colombo Mobsters, Role Models Today, Launching Franchise Stores (The Secret

Sauce? Science). *Forbes*, March 13, www.forbes.com/sites/richardbe-har/2020/03/13/wiseguys-know-pizza-two-former-colombo-mobsters-role-models-today-launching-franchise-stores-the-secret-sauce-science/? sh=51e76265c55e.

Bertone, M. Masoni, C. (2021). *Forme e generi del nuovo racconto criminale*. Soveria Mannella: Rubbettino.

Brayne, S. (2017). Big Data Surveillance: The Case of Policing. *American Sociological Review* 82 (5): 977–1008.

Brewster, T. (2022). How Mexico's Real Life Cartels Recruit Drug Mules on Grand Theft Auto Online, *Forbes*, January 24. www.forbes.com/sites/thomasbrewster/2022/01/24/mexican-cartels-recruit-drug-mules-on-grand-theft-auto-online/?sh=50689969f604.

Button, M., and Cross, C. (2017). *Cyber Frauds, Scams and Their Victims*. London: Routledge.

Caldwell, M., Andrews, J. T. A., Tanay, T., and Griffin L. D. (2020). AI-Enabled Future Crime. *Crime Science* 9 (14). https://doi.org/10.1186/s40163-020-00123-8.

Carrillo, L. (2022). How TikTok Shows Untold Truths of Communities Linked to Drug Trafficking. *Insight Crime*, April 1, https://insightcrime.org/news/how-tiktok-shows-untold-truths-of-communities-linked-to-drug-trafficking/.

Castells, M. (1996). *The Information Age: Economy, Society, and Culture*. Oxford: Blackwell.

Castronova, E. (2014). *Wildcat Currency*. New Haven: Yale University Press.

Catino, M. (2019). *Mafia Organizations*. Cambridge: Cambridge University Press.

Ceccato, V., and Nalla, M. K. (2020). Crime and Fear in Public Places: An Introduction to the Special Issue. *International Journal of Comparative and Applied Criminal Justice* 44: 261–264.

Comolli, V. (2021). Organized Crime during and after the Pandemic. In: C. Varin (ed.), *Global Security in Times of Covid-19: New Security Challenges*. Cham: Palgrave Macmillan. https://doi.org/10.1007/978-3-030-82230-9_11.

Curtis, A. (2011). All watched over by machines of loving grace, *BBC*.

D'Alfonso, S. (2014). A Look at Why Organized Crime and Terror Groups Are Converging. *Security Intelligence*. https://securityintelligence.com/why-organized-crime-and-terror-groups-are-converging/.

Dalby, C. (2021). How Mexico's Cartels Use Video Games to Recruit Children. *InSight Crime*, October 15, https://insightcrime.org/news/mexico-cartels-use-video-games-recruit-new-hitmen/.

Dawkins, R. (1976). *The Selfish Gene*. Oxford: Oxford University Press.

Décary-Hétu, D., and Dupont, B. (2013). Reputation in a Dark Network of Online Criminals. *Global Crime* 14: 175–196.

Di Nicola, A. (2022). Towards Digital Organized Crime and Digital Sociology of Organized Crime. *Trends in Organized Crime*. https://doi.org/10.1007/s12117-022-09457-y.

Direzione Investigativa Antimafia. (2019). *Relazione del Ministro dell'Interno al Parlamento*, direzioneinvestigativaantimafia.interno.gov.it/semestrali/sem/2019/1sem2019.

Eurojust. (2018). *Coordinated Crackdown on 'Ndrangheta Mafia in Europe*, www.eurojust.europa.eu/news/coordinated-crackdown-ndrangheta-mafia-europe.

Europol. (2018). *Internet Organised Crime Threat Assessment*, www.europol.europa.eu/internet-organised-crime-threat-assessment-2018.

Europol. (2019). The GozNym Criminal Network: How It Worked, *Europol*, May 16, www.europol.europa.eu/publications-events/publications/goznym-criminal-network-how-it-worked.

Europol. (2021). Malicious Uses and Abuses of Artificial Intelligence, *Europol*, www.europol.europa.eu/publications-events/publications/malicious-uses-and-abuses-of-artificial-intelligence.

Europol. (2022). *Cryptocurrencies: Tracing the Evolution of Criminal Finances. Europol Spotlight Report Series*. Luxembourg: Publications Office of the European Union.

FBI. (2018). *International Business E-Mail Compromise Takedown*, www.fbi.gov/news/stories/international-bec-takedown-061118.

Fernández-Planells, A., and Orduñez-Malea, E. (2021). Gangs and Social Media: A Systematic Literature Review and an Identification of Future Challenges, Risks and Recommendations. *New Media & Society* 23: 2099–2124.

Fine, G. A. (1983). *Shared Fantasy: Role-Playing Games as Social Worlds*. Chicago: University of Chicago Press.

Follain, J. (2009). *The Last Godfathers: Inside the Mafia's Most Infamous Family*. New York: Thomas Dunne Books.

Frey, T. (2017). 60 Future Crimes That Don't Exist Today, *Future Trends*, June 5, https://futuristspeaker.com/future-trends/60-future-crimes-that-dont-exist-today/.

Gibson, D. C. (2004). *Clues from Killers*. New York: Praeger Publishers.

Glenny, M. (2011). *DarkMarket: Cyberthieves, Cybercops and You*. New York: Knopf.

Glenny, M. (2018). The Cyber Mafia is Growing and Bringing a New Level of Organization to Digital and Internet Crime, *Think: Act Magazine*, December 6, www.rolandberger.com/en/Insights/Publications/Cyber-crime-is-becoming-the-mafia's-newest-racket.html.

Global Initiative against Transnational Organized Crime. (2020). *The Impact of a Pandemic on Organized Crime*, https://globalinitiative.net/wp-content/uploads/2020/03/GI-TOC-Crime-and-Contagion-The-impact-of-a-pandemic-on-organized-crime.pdf.

Gottschalk, P. (2019). Empirical Evidence of Convenience Theory: Reports of Investigations by Fraud Examiners. *Deviant Behavior* 40: 110–121.

Greenberg, A. (2019). Global Takedown Shows the Anatomy of a Modern Cybercriminal Supply Chain, *Wired*, May 16, www.wired.com/story/goznym-takedown-cybercrime-supply-chain/.

Hall, C. (2019). FBI Pulled PlayStation 4 Data to Break Up an Alleged Cocaine Ring, *Polygon*, December 3, www.polygon.com/2019/12/3/20993770/playstation-4-cocaine-ring-fbi-psn-messages.

He, Q, Turel, O, and Bechara, A. (2017). Brain Anatomy Alterations Associated with Social Networking Site (SNS) Addiction, *Scientific Reports*, March 23. https://doi.org/10.1038/srep45064.

Hobsbawm, E. (1959). *Primitive Rebels: Studies in Archaic Forms of Social Movement in the 19th and 20th Centuries*. New York: Norton.

Holgado, Y. H. (2020). Emojis: Criminals Best Friends, *Archyde*, www.archyde.com/emojis-criminals-best-friends/.

Interpol. (2021). *Online African Organized Crime from Surface to Darkweb*. European Union Report.

Jaishankar, K. (ed.). (2011). *Cyber Criminology: Exploring Internet Crimes and Criminal Behavior*. Boca Raton: CRC Press.

Joint Cybercrime Action Taskforce. (2022). Fighting Cybercrime across the World, *Europol*, www.europol.europa.eu/operations-services-and-innovation/services-support/joint-cybercrime-action-taskforce.

Jung, C. (1971). *The Portable Jung*. Harmondsworth: Penguin.

Kampmark, B. (2021). Wither Encryption: What Operation Trojan Shield Reveals, *International Policy Digest*, June 17, https://intpolicydigest.org/wither-encryption-what-operation-trojan-shield-reveals/.

Kefauver, E. (1951). U.S. Senate Special Committee to Investigate Organized Crime in Interstate Commerce, *Kefauver Committee Final Report*, August 31. http://stoppredatorygambling.org/wp-content/uploads/2012/12/Kefauver-Committee-Final-report.pdf.

Kramer, R. (2021). An Examination of Hybrid Organized Criminal Groups' Alliances with Terrorist Groups. *Trends in Organized Crime*. https://doi.org/10.1007/s12117-021-09438-7.

Lavoie, R., Main, K., King, C., and King, D. (2021). Virtual Experience, Real Consequences: The Potential Negative Emotional Consequences of Virtual Reality Gameplay. *Virtual Reality* 25: 69–81.

Lavorgna, A. (2020). *Cybercrimes: Critical Issues in a Global Context*. London: Red Globe Press.

Lavorgna, A., and Antonopoulos, G. A. (2022). Criminal Markets and Networks in Cyberspace. *Trends in Organized Crime* 25: 145–150.

Lembke, A. (2021). *Dopamine Nation*. New York: Dutton.

Leukfeldt, E. R., and Holt, T. J. (2019). Examining the Social Organization Practices of Cybercriminals in the Netherlands Online and Offline. *International Journal of Offender Therapy and Comparative Criminology* 64: https://doi.org/10.1177/0306624X19895886.

Leukfeldt, E. R., Lavorgna, A., and Kleemans, E. R. (2017). Organised Cybercrime or Cybercrime That is Organized? An Assessment of the Conceptualization of Financial Cybercrime as Organised Crime. *European Journal in Criminal Policy and Research* 23: 287–300.

Lunde, P. (2004). *Organized Crime: An Inside Guide to the World's Most Successful Industry*. London: Dorling Kindersley.

Lupo, S. (2009). *The History of the Mafia*. New York: Columbia University Press.

Maalem Lahcen, R. A., Caulkins, B., Mohapatra, R., and Kumar, M. (2020). Review and Insight on the Behavioral Aspects of Cybersecurity. *Cybersecurity* 3 (10). https://doi.org/10.1186/s42400-020-00050-w.

Machiavelli, N. (1513). *The Prince* (Translated by W. K. Marriott). *The Project Gutenberg EBOOK of the Prince*, www.gutenberg.org/files/1232/1232-h/1232-h.htm.

Malinowski, B. (1922). *Argonauts of the Western Pacific*. New York: Dutton.

Maras, M.-H. (2014). *Computer Forensics: Cybercriminals, Laws and Evidence*. Burlington, MA: Jones and Bartlett.

Maras, M.-H. (2016). *Cybercriminology*. Oxford: Oxford University Press.

Marker, M. D. (2017). Organized Crime Has Gone Hight Tech, *Police Chief Magazine*, www.policechiefmagazine.org/organized-crime-has-gone-high-tech/.

McCaffree, K., and Proctor, K. R. (2018). Cocooned from Crime: The Relationship between Video Games and Crime. *Society* 55: 41–52.

McLuhan, M. (1962). *The Gutenberg Galaxy: The Making of Typographic Man*. Toronto: University of Toronto Press.

McLuhan, M. (1964). *Understanding Media: The Extensions of Man*. Cambridge, MA: MIT Press.

McLuhan, M. (1968). *Through the Vanishing Point*. New York: Harper & Row.

McLuhan, M., and Fiore, Q. (1967). *The Medium is the Massage: An Inventory of Effects*. New York: Random House.

McLuhan, M., and McLuhan, E. (1988). *The Laws of Media*. Toronto: University of Toronto Press.

Merriam, C. E. (1915). *Report of the City Council Committee on Crime of the City of Chicago*. Chicago, IL: H. G. Adair.

Milner, R. M. (2016). *The World Made Meme: Public Conversations and Participatory Media*. Cambridge, MA: MIT Press.

Ministero dell'Interno Report 2. (2020). *Permanent Monitoring and Analysis Body on the Risk of Infiltration in the Economy from Mafia-Type Organised Crime*, www.theiacp.org/sites/default/files/Permanent%20Monitoring%20and%20Analysis%20Body%20on%20Organized%20Crime%20Infiltration%20in%20the%20Economy%20after%20COVID_Report%202.pdf.

Moran, T., Kapetaneas, J., and Effron, L. (2019). A Journey through "Hackerville," Romanian City with a Reputation as a Criminal Hacker Breeding Ground, *ABC News*, January 3, https://abcnews.go.com/International/journey-hackerville-romanian-city-reputation-criminal-hacker-breeding/story?id=60123285.

Nicaso, A., and Danesi, M. (2021). *Organized Crime: A Cultural Introduction*. London: Routledge.

Nocera, E. (2021). The Gen-Z Mafia Boss Who Leads His Crew from Beyond the Grave, *Vice*, May 26, www.vice.com/en/article/88nx4b/emanuele-sibillo-mafia-naples.

Nocera, E., and D'Avino, D. (2020). The Italian Mafia Is on TikTok, *Vice*, September 21, www.vice.com/en/article/qj4qxx/the-italian-mafia-is-on-tiktok.

Nolasco Braaten, C., and Vaughan, M. S. (2021). Convenience Theory of Cryptocurrency Crime: A Content Analysis of U.S. Federal Court Decisions. *Deviant Behavior* 42: 958–978.

Norgaard, J., Walbert, H., and Hardy, R. (2018). Shadow Markets and Hierarchies: Comparing and Modeling Networks in the Dark Net. *Journal of Institutional Economics* 14: 877–899.

Operation Wire Wire. (2018). United States Department of Justice, June 11, https://www.justice.gov/opa/pr/74-arrested-coordinated-international-enforcement-operation-targeting-hundreds-individuals.

Paoli, L. (2003). *Mafia Brotherhoods: Organized Crime, Italian Style*. Oxford: Oxford University Press.

Pavlicek, B. (2020). The Cyber Mafia: A Non-Traditional Organized Crime Threat of Pandemic Proportions, *Cybersecurity Magazine*, June 22, https://cybersecurity-magazine.com/the-cyber-mafia-a-non-traditional-organized-crime-threat-of-pandemic-proportions/.

Pieroni, C. (2018). La Crypto Nostra: How Organized Crime Thrives in the Era of Cryptocurrency. *North Carolina Journal of Law & Technology* 20: 111–147.

Quintero, T. L. (2017). The Connected Black Market: How the Dark Web Has Empowered LatAm Organized Crime, *InsightCrime*, https://insight-crime.org/news/analysis/connected-black-market-how-dark-web-empowered-latam-organized-crime/.

Ravveduto, M. (2018). La Google Generation Criminale: I Giovani Della Camorra su Facebook. *Cross* 4: 57–78.

Rees-Mogg, W., and Dale, D. J. (1997). *The Sovereign Individual*. New York: Simon & Schuster.

Renga, D. (2013). *Unfinished Business: Screening the Mafia in the New Millennium*. Toronto: University of Toronto Press.

Revels, A., and Cummings, J. (2014). The Impact of Drug Trafficking on American Indian Reservations with International Boundaries. *The American Indian Quarterly* 38: 287–318.

Reynolds, J. L. (2006). *Shadow People: Inside History's Most Notorious Secret Societies*. Toronto: Key Porter Books.

Royal Canadian Mounted Police. (2022). Dark Web Organized Crime Group Taken Down by BC RCMP FSOC, *Federal Serious & Organized Crime (FSOC)*, https://bc-cb.rcmp-grc.gc.ca/ViewPage.action?siteNodeId=2087&languageId=1&contentId=75127.

Ruggiero, V. (2019). *Organized Crime and Terrorist Networks*. London: Routledge.

Salam, Y., and Moschella, M. (2021). Italian Mafia Fugitive Caught in Dominican Republic After Police Find YouTube Cooking Show, *CNN*, March 30, www.nbcnews.com/news/world/italian-mafia-fugitive-caught-dominican-republic-after-posting-youtube-cooking-n1262435.

Saussure, F. de. (1916). *Cours de linguistique générale*. Paris: Payot.

Scarpinato, R. (2015). Focus on the Mafia's Thinking Mindset. *World Futures* 71: 125–136.

Seal, G. (2009). The Robin Hood Principle: Folklore, History, and the Social Bandit. *Journal of Folklore Research* 46: 67–89.

Sifakis, C. (2005). *Kiss of Death: Mafia Murder Signal. The Mafia Encyclopedia.* New York: Facts On File.

Starbuck, D., Howell, J. C., and Lindquist, D. J. (2001). Hybrid and Other Modern Gangs. *Juvenile Justice Bulletin* (U.S. Department of Justice): 1–8.

Suarez, K. (2021). How Mexican Drug Cartels are Using TikTok to Entice Young People into Organized Crime, *Courier Journal*, January 27, www.courier-journal.com/story/news/2021/01/27/mexican-drug-cartels-using-tiktok-to-entice-young-people/6701080002/.

Sully, M., and Thompson, M. (2010). The Deconstruction of the Mariposa Botnet, *Defence Intelligence*, https://defintel.com/docs/Mariposa_White_Paper.pdf.

Sweeney, O. (2021). Italian Mafia Using Social Media to Reinforce Power, *Euro Weekly*, January 3, https://euroweeklynews.com/2021/01/03/italian-mafia-using-social-media-to-reinforce-power/.

Tal, D. (2020). Future of Organized Crime. *Quantumrun*, www.quantumrun.com/prediction/future-organized-crime-future-crime-p5.

Taylor, T. L. (2006). *Play Between Worlds: Exploring Online Culture.* Cambridge, MA: MIT Press.

Tusikov, N. (2012). The godfather is dead: A hybrid model of organized crime. In: G. Marinez-Salace, S. Vergas Cervantes, and W. Straw (eds.), *Aprehendiendo al Delinquente: Crimen y Medios en el América del Norte.* Kingston: McGill University Press.

United Nations Office on Drugs and Crime. (2004). *United Nations Convention against Transnational Organized Crime and the Protocols Thereto*, www.unodc.org/documents/treaties/UNTOC/Publications/TOC%20Convention/TOCebook-e.pdf.

United Nations Office on Drugs and Crime. (2010). *The Globalization of Crime*, www.unodc.org/documents/data-and-analysis/tocta/TOCTA_Report_2010_low_res.pdf.

United Nations Office on Drugs and Crime. (2013). *World Drug Report*, www.unodc.org/unodc/secured/wdr/wdr2013/World_Drug_Report_2013.pdf.

United Nations Office on Drugs and Crime. (2018). *New Forms of Organized Crime: Networked Structure*, www.unodc.org/e4j/en/organized-crime/module-7/key-issues/networked-structure.html.

United Nations Office on Drugs and Crime. (2019). *Criminal Groups Engaging in Cyber Organized Crime*, www.unodc.org/e4j/zh/cybercrime/module-13/key-issues/criminal-groups-engaging-in-cyber-organized-crime.html.

United Nations Office on Drugs and Crime. (2020). *In Focus: Trafficking over the Darknet – World Drug Report 2020*, www.unodc.org/documents/Focus/WDR20_Booklet_4_Darknet_web.pdf.

Varese, F. (2010). What is organized crime? In: F. Varese (ed.), *Organized Crime: Critical Concepts in Criminology*, 1–33. London: Routledge.

Vavra, S. (2021). The Mafia Finds a New Frontier for Crime: The Internet, *The Daily Beast*, September 23, www.thedailybeast.com/the-mafia-finds-a-new-frontier-for-crime-the-internet.

Walsh, S. (2000). 120 Charged in Probe of Mob on Wall St, *The Washington Post*, June 15, www.washingtonpost.com/archive/politics/2000/06/15/120-charged-in-probe-of-mob-on-wall-st/50ee710e-6e13-4c3e-8b0e-7a47f317bf12/.

Wan, W. (2018). How Emoji Can Kill: As Gangs Move Online, Social Media Fuel Violence, *Washington Post*, www.washingtonpost.com/news/speaking-of-science/wp/2018/06/13/how-emoji-can-kill-as-gangs-move-online-social-media-fuels-violence/.

Weber, J., and Kruisbergen, E. W. (2019). Criminal Markets: The Dark Web, Money Laundering and Counterstrategies – An Overview of the 10th Research Conference on Organized Crime. *Trends in Organized Crime* 22 (1). https://doi.org/10.1007/s12117-019-09365-8.

Weimann, G. (2006). *Terror on the Internet: The New Arena, the New Challenges*. Washington, DC: U.S. Institute of Peace Press.

Wiggins, B. E. (2019). *The Discursive Power of Memes in Digital Culture: Semiotics, Intertextuality, and Ideology*. London: Routledge.

Winder, D. (2017). How Organised Is Organised Cybercrime?, *Raconteur*, December 17. www.raconteur.net/legal/crime/how-organised-is-organised-cybercrime/.

Wise, A. (2010). Mafia Boss Betrayed by Facebook, *ABC News*, March 17, https://abcnews.go.com/International/facebook-finds-mafia-boss/story?id=10124958.

Wray, C. (2018). Digital Transformation: Using Innovation to Combat the Cyber Threat, *FBI News*, March 7, www.fbi.gov/news/speeches/digital-transformation-using-innovation-to-combat-the-cyber-threat.

Zilber, N. (2018). The Rise of Cyber-Mercenaries, *Foreign Policy*, https://foreignpolicy.com/2018/08/31/the-rise-of-the-cyber-mercenaries-israel-nso/.

INDEX

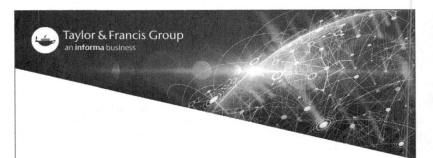